THE SCIENCE & P
OF COACHING S

101
ZONE OFFENSE
PLAYS

Stan Zweifel

COACHES
CHOICE™

ISBN: 1-58518-404-7
Library of Congress Catalog Card Number: 00-108311

Book design: Jeanne Hamilton
Diagrams: Christina Cary
Cover design: Rebecca Gold

Coaches Choice
P.O. Box 1828
Monterey, CA 93942

DEDICATION

This book is dedicated to all my players past and present;
without you guys, we would not be ZONING ON!

ACKNOWLEDGMENTS

Thanks to Dr. Jim Peterson for all his help in my career.

CONTENTS

Dedication 3

Acknowledgments 4

Preface 8

Chapter 1:   Inside Zone Running Plays.................................9

Introduction
- Inside zone blocking rules — footwork 10
- Inside zone blocking rules — covered at the point of attack 11
- Inside zone blocking rules — uncovered at the point of attack 12
- Inside zone blocking rules — center and backside guard combo 12
- Inside zone blocking rules — backside guard and backside tackle combo 13
- Inside zone blocking rules — cutoff block 14
- Inside zone blocking rules — 24/25 zone (TE) concepts, fundamentals, and rules 15

PLAY
1   QUEEN RIGHT 22/23 ZONE TE 19
2   I RIGHT 32/33 ZONE TE SIDE 20
3   QUEEN RIGHT 22/23 BOB SE SIDE 21
4   QUEEN RIGHT 24/25 ZONE TE 22
5   KING RIGHT 24 BACK 23
6   QUEEN RIGHT TWINS Z RIP 24 SMASH 24
7   QUEEN RT 24/25 BOB SE SIDE 25
8   DEUCE RIGHT 24/25 RAZOR TE SIDE 26
9   24/25 BLADE 27
10 DEUCE LEFT H RETURN 25 'O' 28
11 KING RIGHT 24/25 WHAM.. 29
12 DEUCE RIGHT H RIP 24/25 RAZOR SMASH 30
13 TREY RIGHT H LIZ 25 BLADE SMASH 31
14 TREY RIGHT H LEE 22 REVERSE 32
15 TREY LEFT H RAY 23 REVERSE 33
16 TREY RIGHT H LEE 22 34
17 TREY LEFT H RAY 23 35
18 GUN DEUCE RIGHT 24 READ 36

Chapter 2:   Inside Zone Play-Action Passes 37
PLAY
19 QUEEN RIGHT 24/25 NAKED 38
20 QUEEN RIGHT TWINS 24/25 NAKED OUT 39
21 QUEEN RIGHT TWINS 24/25 NAKED CURL 40
22 QUEEN RIGHT TWINS NAKED GO 41
23 QUEEN RIGHT TWINS 24/25 NAKED SCISSORS 42
24 QUEEN RIGHT 24 BOOT 43
25 QUEEN LEFT 24 BOB BOOT 44
26 KING LEFT 25 BACK BOOT 45

CONTENTS

27   QUEEN RIGHT 2401 BACK 46
28   QUEEN RIGTH 2402 47
29   QUEEN RIGHT 2403 48
30   QUEEN RIGHT 2504 49
31   QUEEN LEFT 2505 50
32   QUEEN LEFT 2506 51
33   QUEEN LEFT 2507 52
34   QUEEN LEFT 2508 53
35   QUEEN LEFT 2509 54
36   TRIPS RIGHT 24/25 NAKED STAY 55
37   TREY RIGHT H LEE 22 NEGATIVE 56
38   DUO RIGHT 2400 X QUICK SCREEN LEFT 57
39   DUO RIGHT 2479 58
40   TRIPS LEFT 2400 X SCREEN RIGHT 59

Chapter 3:   Outside Zone Running Plays 61
  •   Split end stretch rules 62
     PLAY
41   QUEEN RIGHT 28/29 SE SIDE 63
42   QUEEN RIGHT Z LIZ 28/29 SEAL SE 64
43   QUEEN RIGHT TWINS 28/29 SE 65
44   QUEEN RIGHT TWINS 28/29 DOUBLE CRACK SE SIDE 66
45   QUEEN RIGHT Z LIZ 28/29 SMASH SE 67
46   QUEEN RIGHT 28/29 CRACK SE 68
47   TRIPS RIGHT 28/29 EDGE SE 69
48   DEUCE RIGHT 28/29 EDGE SE SIDE 70
49   DUO RIGHT F LIZ 28/29 SE SIDE 71
50   TREY RIGHT H LIZ 28/29 SMASH SE SIDE 72
51   TREY RIGHT H LIZ 28/29 SEAL 73
52   QUEEN RIGHT Z LEE 28/29 LEAD SE SIDE 74
  •   Tight end stretch rules 75
53   KING RIGHT 28/29 TE SIDE 76
54   KING RIGHT TWINS Z RIP 28/29 SEAL TE SIDE 77
55   KING RIGHT TWINS Z RIP 28/29 SMASH TE 78
56   KING RIGHT 28/29 CRACK TE SIDE 79
57   KING RIGHT TWINS Z RAY 28/29 LEAD TE 80
58   DEUCE RIGHT 28/29 EDGE TE SIDE 81
59   DUO RIGHT 28/29 EDGE TE 82
60   DEUCE RIGHT H RIP 28/29 TE SIDE 83
61   DUO RIGHT F RETURN 28/29 EDGE TE 84

Chapter 4:   Outside Zone Play-Action Passes 85
     PLAY
62   KING RIGHT 2800/2900 TE 86
63   KING RIGHT 2800/2900 SAIL TE 87
64   DEUCE RIGHT 2800/2900 TE 88
65   QUEEN RIGHT 2900/2800 SE 89
66   QUEEN RIGHT TWINS 2900/2800 THROWBACK SE 90

CONTENTS

67   QUEEN RIGHT 28/29 NAKED SE 91
68   TRIPS RIGHT 29 NAKED OVER 92

Chapter 5:   Option Plays 93
PLAY
69   14/15 TE SIDE 94
70   14/15 G TE SIDE 95
71   14/15 OPEN (SE SIDE ONLY) 96
72   14/15 Z REVERSE 97
73   14/15 OPEN X REVERSE 98
74   18/19 TE 99
75   18/19 SE SIDE 100
76   18/19 STICK TE SIDE 101
77   18/19 STICK SE SIDE 102
78   18/19 Z REVERSE 103
79   18/19 X REVERSE 104
80   18/19 Z REVERSE PASS 105
81   18/19 X REVERSE PASS 106
82   18/19 CRACK SE SIDE 107
83   18/19 CRACK TE SIDE 108
84   18/19 TWINS SE SIDE DOUBLE CRACK 109
85   18/19 TREY FORMATION DOUBLE CRACK 110
86   18/19 TRIPS FORMATION SE SIDE DOUBLE CRACK 111
87   DUO RIGHT 14 G TE SIDE 112
88   DUO LEFT 19 113
89   KING RIGHT F LIZ 19 114
90   QUEEN RIGHT F RIP 18 115
91   DEUCE RIGHT H RIP 18 SEAL TE SIDE 116
92   TREY RIGHT H LIZ 19 SEAL SE SIDE 117
93   ACE 14 G 118

Chapter 6:   Option Play-Action Pass Plays 119
PLAY
94   QUEEN RIGHT 14 G 120
95   QUEEN LEFT TWINS 14 OPEN 121
96   KING RIGHT 18 122
97   QUEEN LEFT TWINS 18 123
98   DUO RIGHT 14 G 124
99   TRIPS LEFT 18 FLOOD 125
100   TRIPS LEFT 18 H SHALLOW 126
101   ACE TREY RIGHT 18 Y SHALLOW 127

ABOUT THE AUTHOR 128

PREFACE

My basic purpose in writing this book is to provide coaches at all levels with an invaluable tool that could help them better understand and implement the *zone offense*. The 101 plays presented in this text are the same plays that we have used successfully for the past nine years at the University of Wisconsin—Whitewater. If they provide coaches with a comparable measure of success, then the time and energy to write this book will have been well worth the effort.

SZ

CHAPTER 1

INSIDE ZONE
RUNNING PLAYS

INTRODUCTION TO INSIDE ZONE PLAYS

Inside zone plays are the heart and soul of a zone offense. As such, inside zone plays encompass the primary basis of a zone offense. The blocking rules presented in this chapter cover all of the assignments on inside zone plays to the tight-end side and the BOB play to the split-end side.

INSIDE ZONE BLOCKING RULES: FOOTWORK

- A wide base should be kept at all times, especially on contact.

- The instep push off allows balance to come from the instep in a flat-footed manner.

- The drop step is designed for a blocker to lose ground to gain a blocking angle and position on a defender. Pick it up and put it down. Depth and width of step is based on the alignment of the defender.

- The drop step allows you too create the best movement on the best angle. You will not shrink the hole because your butt will not be in the hole. You cannot get flattened out or torqued.

- The drop step allows you to cover up a defender on the given angle.

- The drop step creates a slight shoulder turn or shoulder tilt that puts you on the proper angle to cover up the defender. Shoulders tilt and hips open according to how the defender is aligned. Shoulder turn and tilt relative to the defender's alignment. The drop step allows for your second step to get through.

- The second step must get on the ground. How fast can you get the whole foot down?

- The drop step allows you to lower your center of gravity and buys you time to sight the target.

- The drop step allows our lineman to stay gathered by keeping his shoulders between his ankles for balance and demeanor.

- The drop step allows you to lose ground to gain a wider base so that when you strike, you strike with a base.

- The drop step gives you better leverage by lowering your center of gravity and making you strike with stronger posture.

- The drop step allows you the ability to gather yourself and redirect to any inside movement. This demeanor allows you to maintain a base on blocking adjustments.

- Never step underneath yourself or crossover on the second step. If you step underneath yourself, you will shrink the hole.

- The drop step will time up with our running back's alignment, course and chase lane. The running back s must complement our line with the same turn and tilt. The running back will move the defense to influence his decision.

- Most important coaching point: Your shoulders still surge toward the defender; they DO NOT raise up. The upper body goes forward.

- Uncovered drop-step rule: The deeper the linebacker, the deeper your drop step can be.

INSIDE ZONE BLOCKING RULES: COVERED AT THE POINT OF ATTACK

- Assignment: Reach block
  Technique: Drop step, punch and grab
  Target: Two inches outside of midline and get pad under pad

- Drop step and tilt your shoulders on an angle to cover up the defender. Force the defender to make a decision. Stretch, displace, and distort the defender.

- Lead with your helmet, pads, and fist. Let your body go forward and surge on the angle. Punch, lift and strain.

- Cock your arms and whip them for momentum. Thrust with your hands and then grab. Get your arms inside with upper body violence and explosion.

- Get your second step down right away slightly inside the defender's. Knee the defender in the crotch on the crossover and get movement on angle.

- On stalemates, widen your feet quickly, activate your feet, and finish when the defender moves to pursue.

- If the defender slants, stop and drop step with your inside foot to come back and get a piece of him.

- If the defender widens or you feel him beyond your center of gravity, then twist him out with your inside arm and head _ stay on his body and finish. Anticipate redirection inside.

- 90% of the block is finish.

- VERSUS 3 TECHNIQUE
  "Hawk Combo Call"
  Playside guard: Drop step and use playside flipper
  Playside tackle: Lunge off the ball with inside foot (lead step it) and work for surge; drive inside flipper.
  Tight end: solo reach

- VERSUS 4 TECHNIQUE
  "4 Call"
  Playside guard: Drop step, punch, and peak.

Playside tackle: Drop Step, punch, and use flipper; be alert to hand conversion; get movement.

- Assess depth, width, and technique of the defender to establish your split, alignment, and step.

INSIDE ZONE BLOCKING RULES: UNCOVERED AT THE POINT OF ATTACK

- Your drop step is based on the depth of the linebacker. If the linebacker is aligned deep (3-to-5 yards), then take a deeper drop step for depth and width to buy time. If linebacker's depth is less than three yards, then drop step and waddle.

- Versus a slow flow linebacker, key the linebacker. No call requires a bucket step and one-hand technique versus slow-flow linebacker. Punch and grab playside target or utilize flipper technique.

- Versus fast flow linebacker, convert hands to a two-hand punch and peak on the line of scrimmage. (This is our two-hand double team.) Get movement and punch with the outside blocker. Punch extension is crucial.

- The running back must set up your block. Therefore, you have time. An understanding of the timing is crucial. The running back will bring the linebacker to you. Allow the linebacker to press the line of scrimmage. You must understand linebacker play: fill, flow, stem, tuff, etc.

- Maintain shoulder angle and shoulder tilt. Do not get squared up. Be alert to keep your playside arm out. Stair step your alignment. Get off the ball.

- Stay in our demeanor and maintain body control. Understand that the best holes and creases are to the bubble.

INSIDE ZONE BLOCKING RULES: CENTER AND BACKSIDE GUARD COMBO

CENTER

- Versus O technique: normal zone rules apply.

- Versus O technique slant backside: stop, redirect, and put body on defender; maintain shoulder angle and key backside linebacker with eyes; hand conversion to flipper.

- Treat any backside shade as uncovered:

  - Drop step and work bucket progression along the line of scrimmage to the second level. Work your eyes and have a feel for second level timing.

  - On a bucket progression, the backside guard will punch the nose guard into your lap. Be alert to grab it, especially on the slant move.

- No bucket progression on "Hawk Combo Call." Get your eyes on the backside linebacker NOW. Get movement on the double-team combination.

BACKSIDE GUARD

- Versus O technique and uncovered: drop step, punch, and peak; slant away will force you to convert and waddle to second level.

- Versus O technique shaded to the backside: drop step and two-hand it on the playside target; punch and peak. Punch the nose back on the center and get movement. Peak for backside run through. If the linebacker flows fast, finish the nose hard and keep fighting your head inside.

- "Come on" call locks you into a cutoff block.

INSIDE ZONE BLOCKING RULES: BACKSIDE GUARD AND BACKSIDE TACKLE COMBO

- "Under" call or "Mate" call versus 2 technique or 3 technique.

- Assess the alignment of the backside linebacker. You must know if the combo block is versus a Hawk or an Eagle linebacker.

- The backside guard and backside tackle must develop a feel and sense of timing on this play.

BACKSIDE GUARD

- Versus 2 technique: Drop step and two-hand it. If you are ahead of the 2 technique, then let him catch up by stopping or waddling. If you are behind the 2 technique, fight to get your head on the inside target – you still must cover up.

- Versus 3 technique: Treat a 3 technique as if you are uncovered. Bucket step and place your second step in the crotch of the 3 technique. Utilize a flipper technique when blocking half a man. Read the linebacker and feel the defensive line. Hand conversion versus a 3-technique slant. NEVER CROSS OVER!

- Second level adjustment is based on the flow of the Eagle or Hawk linebacker. Insure movement on the double team and keep your playside arm free. Alignment will force a quicker come off, but you must still work it. Eagle alignment will, but you'll have more time for more movement.

- Be alert to "tuff" call versus a slow dog and/or stems.

- Adjust your split to widen the 3 technique.

BACKSIDE TACKLE

- Split and alignment key: minimize and off will help.

- Drop step, and get inside versus a "Hawk" call; two-hand it and fight for movement.

- Can punch and peak versus Hawk linebacker stack.

- Versus "Eagle" call: Drop step punch, and peak; one-hand it while maintaining angle of play. Get second-level linebacker covered on playside number.

- Do NOT get split on this double team combo block. Versus any fast flow linebacker, think hard double team. Two-hand it. Movement is needed to insure cutback crease.

INSIDE ZONE BLOCKING RULES: CUTOFF BLOCK

- -Be alert for BOB versus tight defense.

  -Be alert to High Wall versus penetrator.

  -Be alert to Scoop (with tight end) versus stack.

  -Be alert to TET (with tight end) versus uncovered.

  -Be alert to 5 ON (2 alignment) versus possible slant.

- Adjust split to widen 5 technique or minimize versus 4 technique and 4i technique.

VERSUS 5 TECHNIQUE

- Drop step and utilize backside flipper or rip. Get your second step in the crotch of the 5 technique to keep him wide. Get by the 5 technique, but keep him on your body.

- Butt block if the 5 technique does not cross your face. If you do not feel the defensive lineman on the butt block, then turn your head inside.

VERSUS 4 TECHNIQUE

- Drop step and get your head inside. Stay on the block by beating the 4 technique across the line of scrimmage with your feet. Fight to get by, but stay on the block.

24/25 ZONE (TE) RULES

CONCEPT

- Inside zone blocking play at the 4/5 hole, respectively.

- We can feature to the split-end or tight-end side.

- We are going to sink and drive the ball into the line of scrimmage. The running back will chase the inside leg of the playside tackle as a landmark. The offensive line wants to secure movement along the line of scrimmage, handling slants, stems, and games. We want to create running lanes for the halfback by distorting and displacing the defense. We want the defense to press the line of scrimmage – allow them to be wrong. The offensive line will block zone to the call and double team any look along the line of scrimmage. The halfback will read the first covered lineman playside and feel the rest.

COACHING POINTS

- We will use playside footwork unless we change it. We never want you square – work the angle of the ball. Punch! Punch! Punch!

- The linemen have two rules on this play:

  - Covered (drop step).

  - Uncovered (bucket step).

- Playside covered offensive lineman: Drop step to lower center of gravity – allows you to cover up more efficiently. You will lose ground to gain a position. Drop step, sight the outside number and butt punch. On the second step, "knee the defender in the groin." Do NOT cross over! Block flat-footed to sustain (clown feet). Do NOT allow color to show. Finish: push and pester. Be alert to communicate technique call. We want movement!

- Playside uncovered offensive lineman: You will buy time because of depth. Bucket step based on depth of the linebacker. Key the linebacker on a 3/5/ 9 call. Work the line of scrimmage first; help the adjacent lineman with a one-hand punch. The linebacker must press line of scrimmage. Keep a low center of gravity and work the angle. Do NOT square up on the second level – dip and rip. Versus a 2/4/6/7 call, bucket step and bring your head and hands right now. Your key goes directly to the down lineman. Use a two-handed butt punch to the outside number. Get movement with the adjacent lineman.

CALLS AND ADJUSTMENTS

- Technique calls based on alignment of defenders
- Eagle call (playside)
- Hawk call (playside)
- Under call (backside)
- Backer call (playside to split-end side); second-step decision
- BOB call (playside to split-end side)
- Boss call (playside)
- Bear call (playside); possible "gang" by G.P.
- Man it call (backside) versus 3 technique
- Tight call (backside)

RULES

- Playside tackle rule:

  - 4/5 call (covered rule).

  - Uncovered (uncovered rule); *be alert for 6/7 call from the tight end.

  - Be alert to backer/BOB/Eagle/Hawk call.

  - Work square with a tighter target when covered.

- Playside guard rule:

  - 1/2/3 call (covered rule).

  - Uncovered (uncovered rule); *be alert for 4 call from the offensive tackle.

- Center rule:

  - Shade (covered rule); drop step and bring backside foot to crotch; block the nose guard with your feet; must always get the nose guard to playside number.

  - 0 (covered rule).

  - Shade "in" (covered rule); drop step; hold off for backside guard by sitting down in the duck; work to get movement; keep working.

  - Be alert for "Hawk" call; drop step; and eyeball gap.

- Backside guard rule:
  - Uncovered (uncovered rule).
  - 1 technique (covered rule) drop step.
  - 2/3 technique (uncovered rule) "under" call or "man it" call versus 61 cutoff   *bucket step under.
- Backside tackle rule:
  - Uncovered (uncovered rule) "under" call or "man it" call.
  - 4/5 technique — cutoff (ass block); *be alert for tight adjustment.

    *Note: this is your most important block.

Table 1-1. 24/25 zone (TE) overview.

POSITION	ASSIGNMENT/COACHING POINTS		CALL/ADJUSTMENTS
Playside tackle	4/5 call (covered rule); uncovered (uncovered rule).	Be alert for 6/7 call by the tight.	Be alert for backer/ BOB/Eagle/Hawk Calls.
Playside guard	1/2/3 Call (covered rule); uncovered (uncovered rule).		Be alert for "4 technique" call by the offensive tackle.
Center	"S" shade (covered rule); O technique (covered rule); "W" shade (covered rule).		Be alert for Hawk call. Eyeball A gap line of scrimmage to the second level.
Backside guard	Uncovered (uncovered rule); 1/2 technique (covered rule); 3 technique (uncovered rule).		Be alert for Under Call or man it versus a 2 or 3 technique.
Backside tackle	Uncovered (uncovered rule); 4 technique (drop step and cut); 5 technique (drop and rip).		Be alert for "tight" call; Communicate with the running back.
Tight end	Playside: base block; backside: cut off.	Get movement up the field, then twist; do not allow fold or quick chase.	Be alert for crossing face.
Split end	Playside:man on; backside: near safety.		
Wide receiver	Playside: mano on; backside; near side.		
Quarterback	Open to play call. Drive the ball deep to the half-back; your point of aim is the offensive tackle's inside hip. Open to 10:00 and continue on naked fake after handoff. Six-man rules apply in two-back.		
Halfback	Heels at seven yards. Open step at one and three landmark off the tight end. Second step at playside tackle. Continue on that path playside;feel the rest. If linebackers press, direct your helmet to playside tackle's outside leg.		Chase the playside tackle's inside leg. Sink ball to line of scrimmage at the feet of the offensive line.
Fullback	Heels at five yards. Regardless of position — green or weak, block the first defender outside of offensive tackle.		Read the first covered lineman.

PLAY #1 — "QUEEN RIGHT 22/23 ZONE TE"

4-3

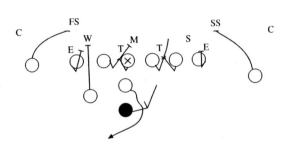

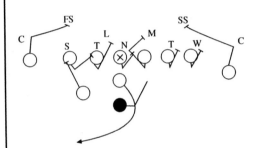

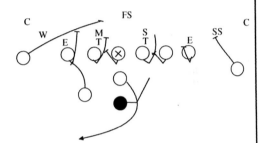

Reduced   Slide Weak

Blocking Rules:

Playside tackle —	Covered rule: tighten target; uncovered: switch footwork double with PSG.
Playside guard —	Covered rule (1/2): double with center (3 tech), double with tackle; uncovered: tighten target.
Center —	Shade strong covered; uncovered: shade weak; work backside guard.
Backside guard —	Covered rule: under; uncovered rule: get movement; don't come off unless the linebacker is level.
Backside tackle —	Uncovered: under call, 4 technique; drop and rip.
Tight end —	Tight target.

Backfield Coaching Points:

Z —	Near safety.
X —	Near safety.
FB —	Vs. stack: under call, 4-3 man it.
TB —	Chase the inside of leg of the playside guard, hit it north/south
QB —	Open to 6 O'clock: seat the ball quickly with eyes; continue on naked course.

PLAY # 2 — "I RIGHT 32/33 ZONE TE SIDE"

4-3

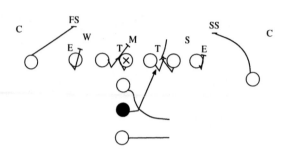

Reduced

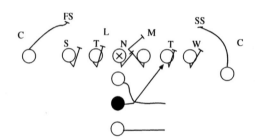

Slide Weak

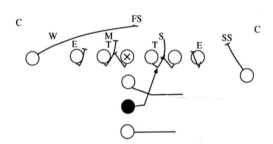

Blocking Rules:

Playside tackle —	Same as 22/23.
Playside guard —	Same as 22/23.
Center —	Same as 22/23.
Backside guard —	Same as 22/23.
Backside tackle —	Same as 22/23.
Tight end —	Same as 22/23.

Backfield Coaching Points:

Z —	Near safety.
X —	Near safety.
FB —	Heels at five yards; J step; second step at inside leg of PSG; read first covered lineman; think cutback.
TB —	Get in option phase.
QB —	Get ball as deep and as quickly as possible to the FB; get your hips out of hole; continue the option phase.

PLAY # 3 — "QUEEN RIGHT 22/23 BOB SE SIDE"

4-3

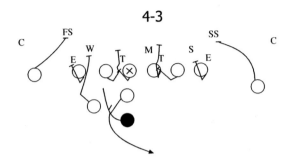

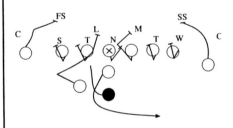

Reduced

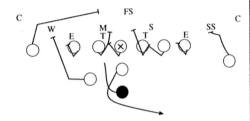

Slide Weak

Blocking Rules:

Playside tackle — Covered: reach the outside number.

Playside guard — Covered: reach the outside number; uncovered: zone first to second level.

Center — Covered reach outside number; uncovered: zone first to second level.

Backside guard — Covered: under/cutoff; uncovered: zone first to second level.

Backside tackle — Covered: cutoff; uncovered: under.

Tight end — Cutoff.

Backfield Coaching Points:

Z — Near safety.

X — Near safety.

FB — Step outside to sell 28/29; read first covered lineman to linebacker.

TB — Heels at seven yards; drop step; chase the inside of the PSG; reach the 3 technique or shade.

QB — Front out; drive the ball deep to the tailback; continue on naked path.

PLAY #4 — "QUEEN RIGHT 24/25 ZONE TE"

4-3

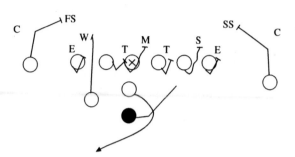

Reduced

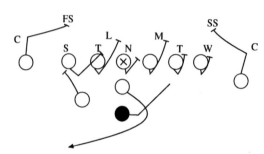

Slide Weak

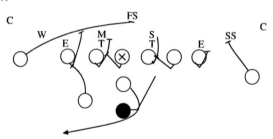

Blocking Rules:

Playside tackle —	Block 24/25 zone rules.
Playside guard —	Block 24/25 zone rules.
Center —	Block 24/25 zone rules.
Backside guard —	Block 24/25 zone rules.
Backside tackle —	Block 24/25 zone rules.
Tight end —	Block 24/25 zone rules.

Backfield Coaching Points:

Z —	Block near safety.
X —	Block near safety.
FB —	Block first defender on the outside of the off tackle; vs. 4-3 man it call.
TB —	Heels at seven yards; open step at first and third landmark off TE; chase the inside leg of the PST; sink the ball; fell the rest.
QB —	Open to 10:00; get the ball deep to the TB and continue on naked fake.

4-3

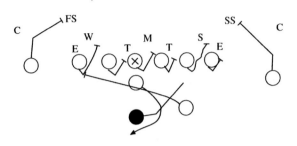

Reduced

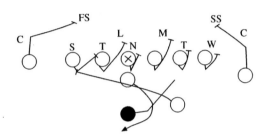

Slide Weak

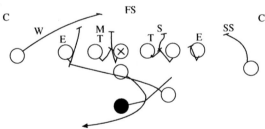

Blocking Rules:

Playside tackle —	Block 24/25 zone rules.
Playside guard —	Block 24/25 zone rules.
Center —	Block 24/25 zone rules.
Backside guard —	Block 24/25 zone rules.
Backside tackle —	Block 24/25 zone rules.
Tight end —	Block 24/25 zone rules.

Backfield Coaching Points:

Z —	Near safety.
X —	Near safety.
FB —	Same as 24/25 zone.
TB —	Same as 24/25 zone.
QB —	Same as 24/25 zone.

PLAY # 6 — "QUEEN RIGHT TWINS Z RIP 24 SMASH"

4-3

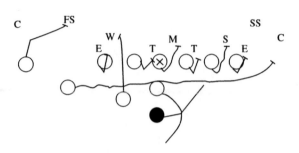

Reduced

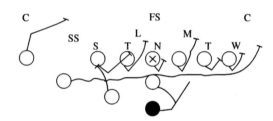

Slide Weak

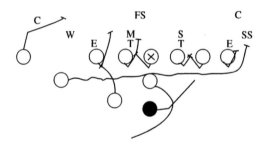

Blocking Rules:

Playside tackle —	Block 24/25 zone rules.
Playside guard —	Block 24/25 zone rules.
Center —	Block 24/25 zone rules.
Backside guard —	Block 24/25 zone rules.
Backside tackle —	Block 24/25 zone rules.
Tight end —	Block 24/25 zone rules.

Backfield Coaching Points:

Z —	Rip motion block the first wrong colored jersey outside of the TE's alignment.
X —	Near safety.
FB —	Same as 24/25 zone.
TB —	Same as 24/25 zone.
QB —	Same as 24/25 zone.

PLAY #7 — "QUEEN RIGHT 24/25 BOB SE SIDE"

4-3

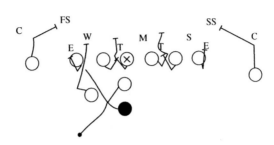

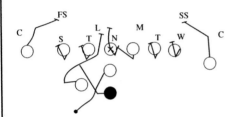

Reduced

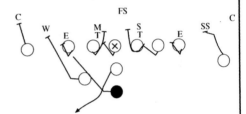

Slide Weak

Blocking Rules:

Playside tackle —	Covered: reach outside number; Uncovered: backer call and technique.
Playside guard —	Covered: reach outside number; uncovered: zone first to second level.
Center —	Covered: reach outside number; uncovered: zone first to second level.
Backside guard —	Covered: under; cutoff; uncovered: zone first to second level.
Backside tackle —	Covered; cut-off; uncovered: under.
Tight end —	Backside cutoff.

Backfield Coaching Points:

Z —	Near safety.
X —	Near safety.
FB —	Step outside to sell 28/29; read the first colored lineman playside to plug the linebacker.
TB —	Second step at the inside leg of the tackle; read the 3 or 5 technique.
QB —	Front out to the tailback; drive the ball deep; continue on 2400/2500 fake.

PLAY #8 — "DEUCE RIGHT 24/25 RAZOR TE SIDE"

4-3

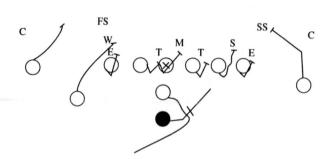

Reduced

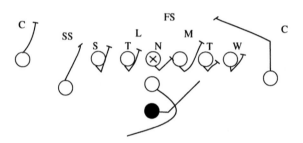

Slide Weak

Blocking Rules:

Playside tackle — Block 24/25 zone rules.

Playside guard — Block 24/25 zone rules.

Center — Block 24/25 zone rules.

Backside guard — Block 24/25 zone rules.

Backside tackle — Stay on man; work your path.

Tight end — Block 24/25 zone rules.

Backfield Coaching Points:

Z— Near safety.

X — Block the outside 1/3 defender.

Mustang — Radical inside release; block the most dangerous man.

TB — Run 24/25 zone.

QB — Run 24/25 zone.

4-3

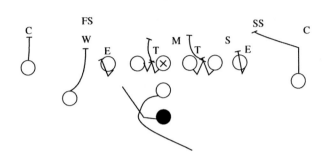

Reduced

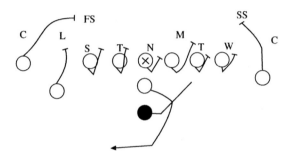

Slide Weak

Blocking Rules:	**Backfield Coaching Points:**
Playside tackle — Block 24/25 zone rules.	Z — Near safety.
Playside guard — Block 24/25 zone rules.	X — Man responsible for outside 1/3 on cover 2; block the corner.
Center — Block 24/25 zone rules.	
Backside guard — Block 24/25 zone rules.	Mustang — Block the most dangerous man.
Backside tackle — Block 24/25 zone rules.	TB— Run 24/25 BOB.
Tight end — Block 24/25 zone rules.	QB — Run 24/25 BOB.

4-3

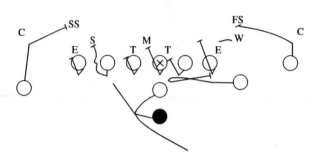

Reduced

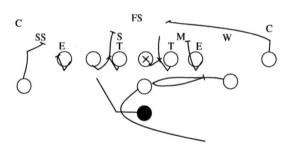

Slide Weak

Blocking Rules:

Playside tackle —	Block 24/25 zone rules.
Playside guard —	Block 24/25 zone rules.
Center —	Block 24/25 zone rules.
Backside guard —	Block 24/25 zone rules.
Backside tackle —	Sift to second level; return motion will block the backside edge.
Tight end —	Block 24/25 zone rules.

Backfield Coaching Points:

Z —	Near safety.
X —	Near safety.
Mustang —	Run motion to the center and return towards original alignment; the ball is snapped so you can block the C gap edge.
TB —	Run 24/25.
QB —	Run 24/25.

PLAY # 11 — "KING RIGHT 24/25 WHAM"

4-3

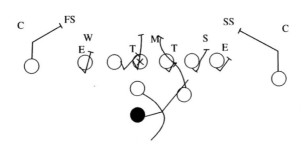

Reduced

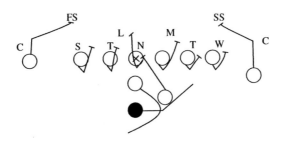

Slide Weak

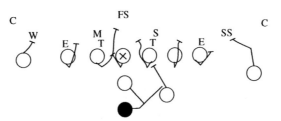

Blocking Rules:

Playside tackle — Block 24/25 zone rules.

Playside guard — Block 24/25 zone rules.

Center — Covered: blunt first or second level; uncovered: block 24/25 zone.

Backside guard — Covered: cutoff; uncovered: zone first to second level.

Backside tackle — Covered: cutoff.

Tight end — Block 24/25 zone rules.

Backfield Coaching Points:

Z — Near safety.

X — Near safety.

FB — Attack line of scrimmage; block on the LOS.

TB — Run 24/25.

QB — Run 24/25.

PLAY # 12 — "DEUCE RIGHT H RIP 24/25 RAZOR SMASH"

4-3

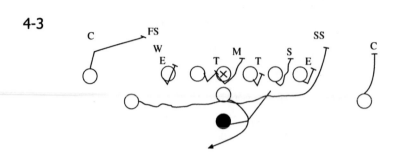

Reduced

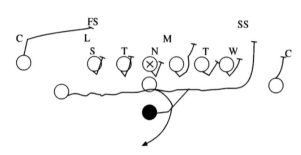

Slide Weak

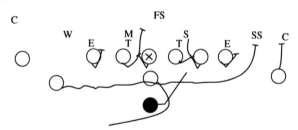

Blocking Rules:

Playside tackle — Block 24/25 zone rules.

Playside guard — Block 24/25 zone rules.

Center — Block 24/25 zone rules.

Backside guard — Block 24/25 zone rules.

Backside tackle — Stay on man; work your path vertical.

Tight end — Block 24/25 zone rules.

Backfield Coaching Points:

Z — Near safety.

X — Near safety.

Mustang — Motion right; block first wrong colored jersey outside of TE.

TB — Run 24/25.

QB — Run 24/25.

PLAY #13 — "TREY RIGHT H LIZ 25 BLADE SMASH"

4-3

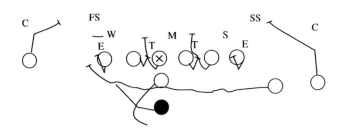

Reduced

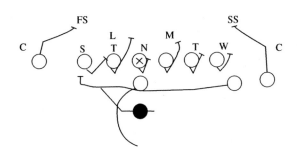

Slide Weak

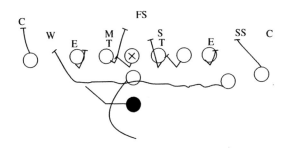

Blocking Rules:		Backfield Coaching Points:	
Playside tackle —	Block 24/25 BOB.	Z —	Near safety.
Playside guard —	Block 24/25 BOB.	X —	Block man responsible for outside 1/3; cover 2 block corner.
Center —	Block 24/25 BOB.		
Backside guard —	Block 24/25 BOB.	Mustang —	Block most dangerous man.
Backside tackle —	Block 24/25 BOB.	TB —	Run 24/25 BOB.
Tight end —	Block 24/25 BOB.	QB —	Run 24/25 BOB.

PLAY # 14 — "TREY RIGHT H LEE 22 REVERSE"

4-3

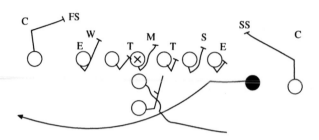

Reduced

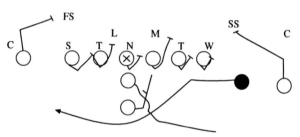

Slide Weak

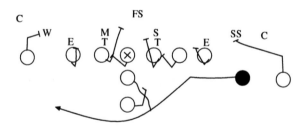

Blocking Rules:

Playside tackle — Block 24/25 zone rules.

Playside guard — Block 24/25 zone rules.

Center — Block 24/25 zone rules.

Backside guard — Block 24/25 zone rules.

Backside tackle — Zone to second level; let edge go.

Tight end — Block 24/25 zone rules.

Backfield Coaching Points:

Z — Radical inside release block near safety.

X — Push crack block.

Mustang — Orbit motion time your motion to receive ball from QB.

TB — Run 22/23.

QB — Quick fake to TB; hand to mustang back on 29 path; carry out negative fake.

PLAY #15 — "TREY LEFT H RAY 23 REVERSE"

4-3

Reduced

Slide Weak

Blocking Rules:

Playside tackle — Block 22/23 zone rules.

Playside guard — Block 22/23 zone rules.

Center — Block 22/23 zone rules.

Backside guard — Block 22/23 zone rules.

Backside tackle — Zone to second level; let the edge go.

Tight end — Block 22/23 zone.

Backfield Coaching Points:

Z — Near safety.

X — Push crack.

Mustang — Orbit motion be in position to receive ball from QB.

TB — Run 22/23.

QB — Quick fake to TB; hand to mustang back on 28 path; carry out negative fake.

PLAY #16 — "TREY RIGHT H LEE 22"

4-3

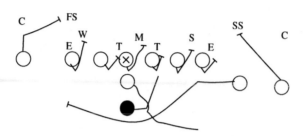

Reduced

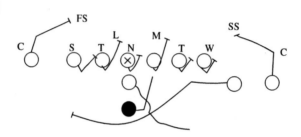

Slide Weak

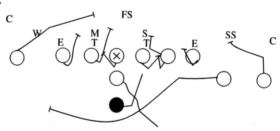

Blocking Rules:

Playside tackle — Block 22/23 zone rules.

Playside guard — Block 22/23 zone rules.

Center — Block 22/23 zone rules.

Backside guard — Block 22/23 zone rules.

Backside tackle — Sift to second level unless two men are on LOS, then base block.

Tight end — Block 22/23 zone rules.

Backfield Coaching Points:

Z — Near safety.

X — Near safety.

Mustang — Orbit motion; take fake from QB on 28/29 path.

TB — Run 22/23 zone.

QB — Hand to TB; fake 28/29 to mustang back.

PLAY # 17 — "TREY LEFT H RAY 23"

4-3

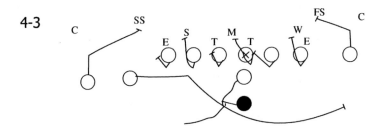

Reduced

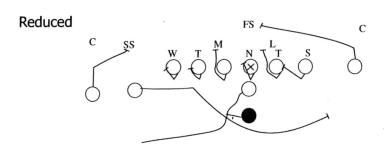

Slide Weak

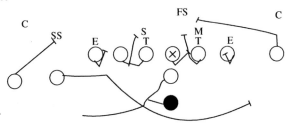

Blocking Rules:

Playside tackle —	Block 22/23 zone.
Playside guard —	Block 22/23 zone.
Center —	Block 22/23 zone.
Backside guard —	Block 22/23 zone.
Backside tackle —	Sift to second level unless two men on LOS, then base man on.
Tight end —	Block 22/23 zone.

Backfield Coaching Points:

Z —	Near safety.
X —	Near safety.
Mustang —	Orbit motion; receive fake for 28/29 path.
TB —	Run 22/23 zone.
QB —	Run 22/23; fake 28/29 to mustang back.

PLAY #18 — "GUN DEUCE RIGHT 24 READ"

4-3

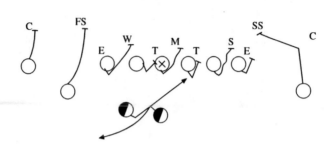

Reduced

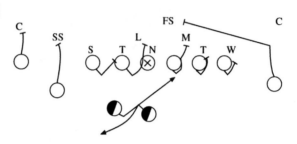

Slide Weak

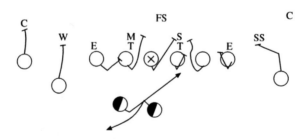

Blocking Rules:

Playside tackle —	Block 24 zone.
Playside guard —	Block 24 zone.
Center —	Block 24 zone.
Backside guard —	Block 24 zone.
Backside tackle —	Sift to second level.
Tight end —	Sift to second level.

Backfield Coaching Points:

Z —	Block defender over you.
X —	Block defender over you.
Mustang —	Block defender over you.
TB —	Run 24; if QB gives you the ball know cutback should be there, if QB keeps, give good fake.
QB —	Take gun snap; read weakside 5 technique; if he works upfield, hand the ball to TB; if he closes, keep the ball, and run.

CHAPTER 2

INSIDE ZONE
PLAY-ACTION PLAYS

PLAY # 19 — "QUEEN RIGHT 24/25 NAKED

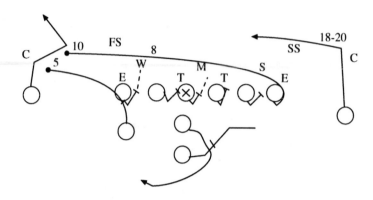

Blocking Rules:

Playside tackle — Block 24/25 rules; block the first level with your hands, and the second level with your eyes looking for the linebacker to run through.

Playside guard — Block 24/25 rules; block the first level with your hands, and the second level with your eyes looking for the linebacker.

Center — Block 24/25 rules; block the first level with your hands, and the second level with your eyes looking for the linebacker.

Backside guard — Block 24/25 rules; block the first level with your hands, and the second level with your eyes looking for the linebacker.

Backside tackle — Block 24/25 rules; block the first level with your hands, and the second level with your eyes looking for the linebacker.

Tight end — First step to the outside to simulate 24/25; run a crossing route from 8-10 yards depth.

Backfield Coaching Points:

Z — Come open late at 18-20 yards depth.

X — Post corner.

FB — Blunt edge – release to flat at five yards.

TB — Fake 24/25 on third step; throw hand to outside hip and veer towards sidelines.

QB — Fake 24/25; get depth and width vs. cover 2; high to low vs. cover 1-4-8-3 low to high.

PLAY #20 — "QUEEN RIGHT TWINS 24/25 NAKED OUT

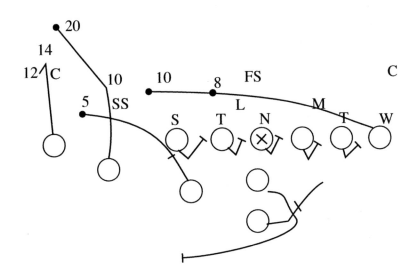

Blocking Rules:

Playside tackle —	Block 24/25 rules; block first level with your hands, and the second level with your eyes looking for the linebacker to run through.
Playside guard —	Block 24/25 rules; block first level with your hands, and the second level with your eyes looking for the linebacker.
Center —	Block 24/25 rules; block first level with your hands, and the second level with your eyes looking for the linebacker.
Backside guard —	Block 24/25 rules; block first level with your hands, and the second level with your eyes looking for the linebacker.
Backside tackle —	Block 24/25 rules; block first level with your hands, and the second level with your eyes looking for the linebacker.
Tight end —	First step outside to simulate 24/25; run a crossing route from 8-10 yards depth.

Backfield Coaching Points:

Z —	Run a complimentary route for out descriptor; sail cut 10 to 20 yards.
X —	Descriptor tells you to run a cornerback out at 14 to 12.
FB —	Blunt edge; release to flat at five yards.
TB —	24/25 naked rules.
QB —	24/25 naked rules.

PLAY #21 — "QUEEN RIGHT TWINS 24/25 NAKED CURL"

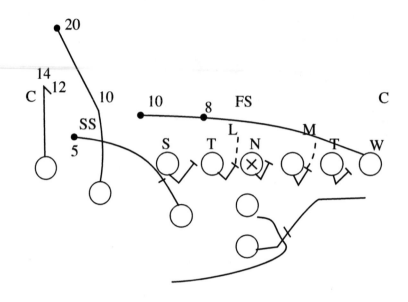

Blocking Rules:

Playside tackle —	24/25 naked rules.
Playside guard —	24/25 naked rules.
Center —	24/25 naked rules.
Backside guard —	24/25 naked rules.
Backside tackle —	24/25 naked rules.
Tight end —	24/25 naked route.

Backfield Coaching Points:

Z —	Run a complimentary route for curl; sail route at 10 to 20 yards.
X —	Run called route – curl at 14 to 12 yards.
FB —	Blunt edge – flat at five yards.
TB —	Fake 24/25.
QB —	24/25 naked route.

PLAY #22 — "QUEEN RIGHT TWINS NAKED GO"

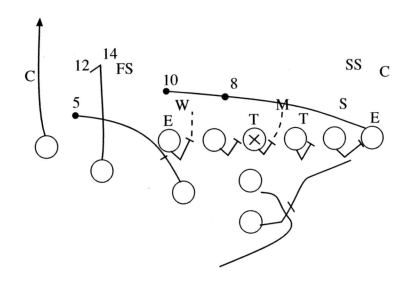

Blocking Rules:

Playside tackle —	24/25 naked rules.
Playside guard —	4/25 naked rules.
Center —	24/25 naked rules.
Backside guard —	24/25 naked rules.
Backside tackle —	24/25 naked rules.
Tight end —	Crossing route 8-10 yards.

Backfield Coaching Points:

Z —	Complimentary route comeback at 14 -to- 12 yards.
X —	Go route.
FB —	24/25 naked route.
TB —	Fake 24/25.
QB —	24/25 naked route.

PLAY #23 — "QUEEN RIGHT TWINS 24/25 NAKED SCISSORS"

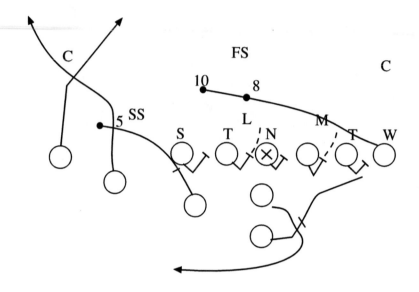

Blocking Rules:

Playside tackle —	24/25 naked rules.
Playside guard —	24/25 naked rules.
Center —	24/25 naked rules.
Backside guard —	24/25 naked rules.
Backside tackle —	24/25 naked rules.
Tight end —	Crossing route 8-10 yards.

Backfield Coaching Points:

Z —	Run a bend corner cut going under X.
X —	Run a skinny post – going over Z's route.
FB —	Flat at five yards.
TB —	Fake 24/25.
QB —	Fake 24/25.

PLAY #24 — "QUEEN RIGHT 24 BOOT"

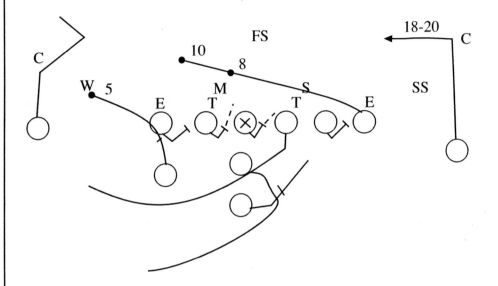

Blocking Rules:

Playside tackle —	Block 24/25.
Playside guard —	Pull and log first wrong colored jersey outside of split tackle.
Center —	Secure frontside A gap; if no down lineman in frontside A, flatten out for pulling guard.
Backside guard —	Block 24/25.
Backside tackle —	Block 24/25.
Tight end —	Crossing route 8-10 yards.

Backfield Coaching Points:

Z —	Come open late.
X —	Post corner.
FB —	Blunt edge; flat at five yards.
TB —	Fake 24/25; help fill B Gap.
QB —	Fake 24/25; read progression.

PLAY #25 — "QUEEN LEFT 24 BOB BOOT"

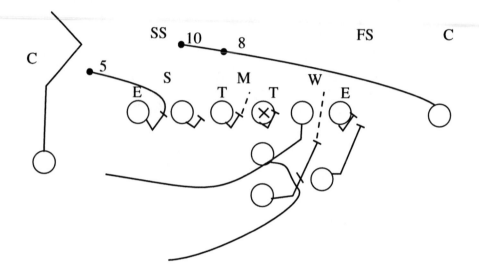

Blocking Rules:

Playside tackle —	Block 24/25 BOB.
Playside guard —	Pull and log first wrong colored jersey outside of split tackle.
Center —	Block 24/25 BOB.
Backside guard —	Block 24/25 BOB.
Backside tackle —	Block 24/25 BOB.
Tight end —	Step inside to simulate 24/25 BOB; release flat gaining width to a depth of five yards.

Backfield Coaching Points:

Z —	Post corner.
X —	Close split run crossing route at 8-10 yards.
FB —	Fake 24/25 BOB; block D gap.
TB —	Fake 24/25 BOB; fill B gap.
QB —	Fake 24/25 BOB; break contain 2; read high to low, cover 1-2-8-3 low to high.

PLAY #26 — "KING LEFT 25 BACK BOOT"

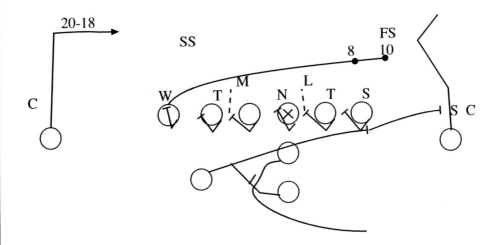

Blocking Rules:

Playside tackle —	Block 24/25 zone.
Playside guard —	Pull and log first wrong colored jersey outside of split tackle.
Center —	Pull and log first wrong colored jersey outside of split tackle.
Backside guard —	Pull and log first wrong colored jersey outside of split tackle.
Backside tackle —	Pull and log first wrong colored jersey outside of split tackle.
Tight end —	Crossing route at 8-10 yards.

Backfield Coaching Points:

Z—	Come open late at 18-to-20 yards.
X —	Post corner.
FB —	Come under QB; blunt edge release to flat at depth of five yards.
TB —	Fake 24/255.
QB—	Fake 24/25; read coverage progression.

PLAY #27 — "QUEEN RIGHT 2401 BACK"

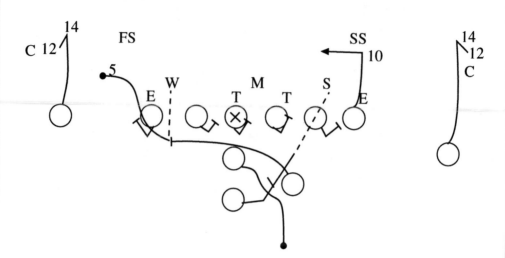

Blocking Rules:

Playside tackle —	Covered: pass pro man; uncovered: pass pro man on TE.
Playside guard —	Covered: pass pro man; uncovered: work inside linebacker with the center.
Center —	Frontside shade: work the inside linebacker with playside guard; uncovered: work backside.
Backside guard —	Covered: pass pro man; uncovered: work with inside linebacker with the center.
Backside tackle —	Pass pro man on.
Tight end —	Best possible release — run a 10-yard square in.

Backfield Coaching Points:

Z —	Run a 14-to-12 yard out.
X —	Run a 14-to-12 yard out.
FB —	Run course under QB; you are responsible for the Will backer; then check option out five yards.
TB —	Great 24/25 fake; then check Sam or 3 linebacker; set on 2 linebacker; set check Mike.
QB —	Fake 24/25; 5-step drop set behind P.S.T.; strongside: drop of SS weak – drop of Will.

PLAY #28 — "QUEEN RIGHT 2402"

Blocking Rules:

Playside tackle —	Covered: pass pro man on; uncovered: pass block man on TE.
Playside guard —	Covered: pass pro man on; uncovered: work inside linebacker with the center.
Center —	Frontside shade: work inside linebacker with PSG; uncovered: work backside.
Backside guard —	Covered: pass pro man; uncovered: work inside linebacker with the center.
Backside tackle —	Pass pro man on.
Tight end —	Best possible release —run a 10-yard out.

Backfield Coaching Points:

Z —	Run a 14-to-12 yard comeback out.
X —	Run a 14-to-12 yard comeback out.
FB —	Responsible for Will backer; if he drops, run a 5-yard check option.
TB —	Responsible for Sam on three linebacker set; responsible for Mike on two-linebacker set.
QB —	Fake 24/25; 3-deep/best matchup; strongside: drop of SS; weakside drop of Will.

PLAY #29 — "QUEEN RIGHT 2403"

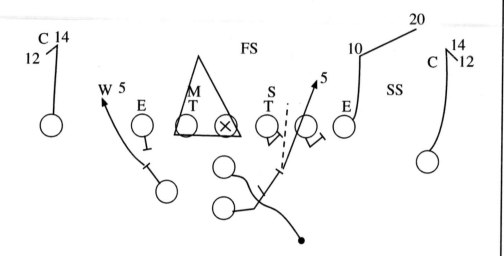

Blocking Rules:

Playside tackle —	Block 2400/2500 rules.
Playside guard —	Block 2400/2500 rules.
Center —	Block 2400/2500 rules.
Backside guard —	Block 2400/2500 rules.
Backside tackle —	Block 2400/2500 rules.
Tight end —	Best possible release — run a sail route with the first cut at 10 yards, angled to a depth of 20 yards.

Backfield Coaching Points:

Z —	14 -to-12 yard comeback out.
X —	14 -to-12 yard comeback out.
FB —	Check option.
TB —	Fake 24/25.
QB —	Fake 24/25; strongside: drop of strong corner; weakside: drop of Will linebacker.

PLAY #30 —"QUEEN LEFT 2504"

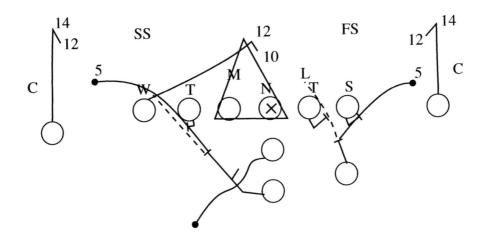

Blocking Rules:

Playside tackle — Block 2400/2500.

Playside guard — Block 2400/2500.

Center — Block 2400/2500.

Backside guard — Block 2400/2500.

Backside tackle — Block 2400/2500.

Tight end — Inside release — run a 12-10 yard curl.

Backfield Coaching Points:

Z — 14-to-12 yard curl.

X — 14-to-12 yard curl.

FB — Check flat.

TB — Fake 24/25; check flat.

QB — Fake 24/25; vs. zone, read squeeze of inside linebackers; vs. man receivers, convert to digs.

PLAY #31— "QUEEN LEFT 2505"

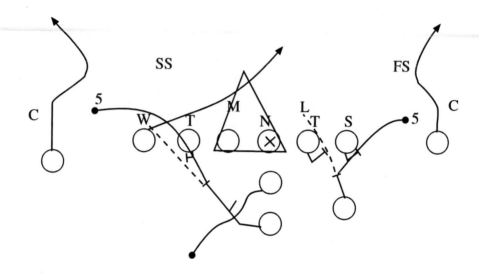

Blocking Rules:

Playside tackle —	Block 2400/2500.
Playside guard —	Block 2400/2500.
Center —	Block 2400/2500.
Backside guard —	Block 2400/2500.
Backside tackle —	Block 2400/2500.
Tight end —	Inside release, run centerfield; split the field in half.

Backfield Coaching Points:

Z —	Post corner.
X —	Post corner.
FB —	Check flat.
TB —	Fake 24/25; check flat.
QB —	Fake 24/25; vs. 2-deep, read near half field safety; vs. man, best matchup.

PLAY #32 — "QUEEN LEFT 2506"

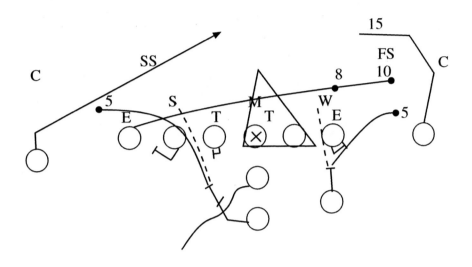

Blocking Rules:

Playside tackle —	Block 2400/2500.
Playside guard —	Block 2400/2500.
Center —	Block 2400/2500.
Backside guard —	Block 2400/2500.
Backside tackle —	Block 2400/2500.
Tight end —	Run a crossing route at 8-10 yards; sit vs. zone; stay on move vs. man.

Backfield Coaching Points:

Z —	Skinny post.
X —	Post dig route at 15 yards.
FB —	Check flat.
TB —	Fake 24/25; check flat.
QB —	Fake 24/25; vs. zone, weakside hook to dig; vs. man, TE to X.

PLAY #33 — "QUEEN LEFT 2507"

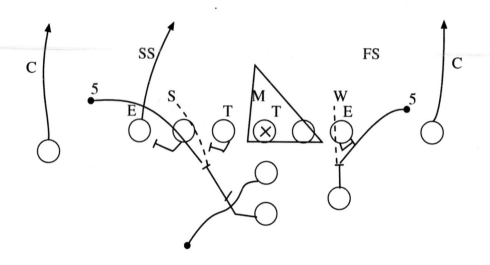

Blocking Rules:

Playside tackle —	Block 2400/2500.
Playside guard —	Block 2400/2500.
Center —	Block 2400/2500.
Backside guard —	Block 2400/2500.
Backside tackle —	Block 2400/2500.
Tight end —	Best possible route is to run a vertical take-off; keep spacing, do not get rerouted.

Backfield Coaching Points:

Z —	Vertical take-off; work seven yards from sideline.
X —	Vertical take-off route; work seven yards from sideline.
FB —	Check flat.
TB —	Fake 24/25; check flat.
QB —	Fake 24/25; best possible match up.

PLAY #34 — "QUEEN LEFT 2508"

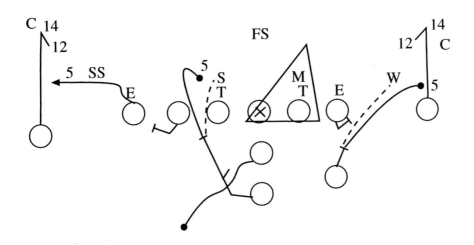

Blocking Rules:

Playside tackle —	Block 2400/2500.
Playside guard —	Block 2400/2500.
Center —	Block 2400/2500.
Backside guard —	Block 2400/2500.
Backside tackle —	Block 2400/2500.
Tight end —	Run a 5-yard flat.

Backfield Coaching Points:

Z —	Run a 14-to-12 yard stop hook.
X —	Run a 14-to-12 yard stop hook.
FB —	Check flat at five yards.
TB —	Fake 24/25; check circle at five yards.
QB —	Fake 24/25; vs. 3-deep, strong curl to strong flat; vs. 2-deep, read weak curl.

PLAY #35 — "QUEEN LEFT 2509"

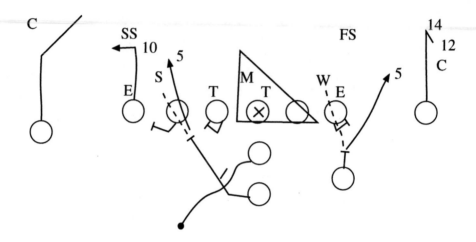

Blocking Rules:

Playside tackle —	Block 2400/2500.
Playside guard —	Block 2400/2500.
Center —	Block 2400/2500.
Backside guard —	Block 2400/2500.
Backside tackle —	Block 2400/2500.
Tight end —	Run a 10-yard out.

Backfield Coaching Points:

Z —	Run a skinny post.
X —	14-to-12 comeback out.
FB —	Check option.
TB —	Fake 24/25; check option.
QB —	Fake 24/25; vs. 3-deep, X to option; vs. 2 deep, post; vs. man, post to out.

PLAY #36— "TRIPS RIGHT 24/25 NAKED STAY"

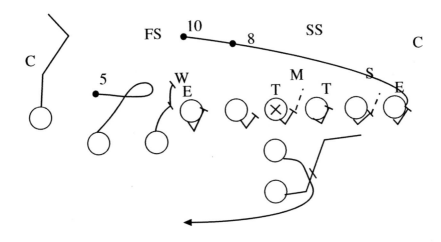

Blocking Rules:

Playside tackle —	Block 2400/2500.
Playside guard —	Block 2400/2500.
Center —	Block 2400/2500.
Backside guard —	Block 2400/2500.
Backside tackle —	Block 2400/2500.
Tight end —	Step for 24/25; run a crossing route at 8-10 yards.

Backfield Coaching Points:

Z —	Run a pivot arrow at five yards.
X —	Run a post corner route.
Mustang —	Pin the first wrong colored jersey in the C gap up to second level.
TB —	Fake 24/25.
QB —	Fake 24/25; break contain on run/pass option; vs. cover 2, high to low; vs. other coverages low to high.

PLAY #37 "TREY RIGHT H LEE 22 NEGATIVE"

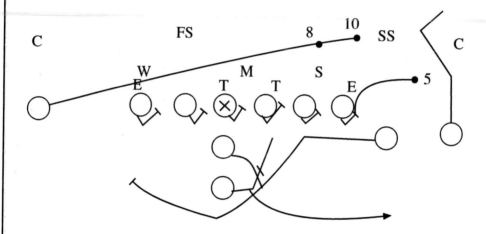

Blocking Rules:

Playside tackle —	Block 22/23 rules.
Playside guard —	Block 22/23 rules.
Center —	Block 22/23 rules.
Backside guard —	Block 22/23 rules.
Backside tackle —	Block 22/23 rules.
Tight end —	Block 22; release into the flat; find the voided areas.

Backfield Coaching Points:

Z —	Run a post - corner route.
X —	Run a come open late at 18-20 yards.
Mustang —	Orbit motion left; fake 22 reverse; block first wrong colored jersey to show.
TB —	Fake 22/23; get tackled.
QB —	Fake 22/23; break contain; read low to high; vs. 2 cover, high to low.

Blocking Rules:

Playside tackle —	Block 24/25 rules.
Playside guard —	Block 24/25 rules.
Center —	Block 24/25 rules.
Backside guard —	Block 24/25 rules.
Backside tackle —	Work a vertical path vs. man on.
Tight end —	Block 24/25.

Backfield Coaching Points:

Z —	Block the most dangerous man.
X —	Jab step; receive screen pass; read block of the Z.
FB —	Wing position block 24/25.
TB —	Fake 24/25.
QB —	Open one step; show ball for 24/25 fake; whirl and throw a forward pass to X.

PLAY # 39 — "DUO RIGHT 2479"

Blocking Rules:

Playside tackle —	Block 24/25 rules.
Playside guard —	Block 24/25 rules.
Center —	Block 24/25 rules.
Backside guard —	Block 24/25 rules.
Backside tackle —	Block 24/25 rules.
Tight end —	Read route; breaking is point at 10-yard out or sail.

Backfield Coaching Points:

Z —	Slant route at four yards.
X —	Slant route at six yards.
FB —	Wing position; run a speed flat cut a 5-yard gain width before depth.
TB —	Fake 24/25.
QB —	Fake 24/25; set up behind PST; read strong flat-to-strong hook area.

PLAY #40 — "TRIPS LEFT 2400 X SCREEN RIGHT"

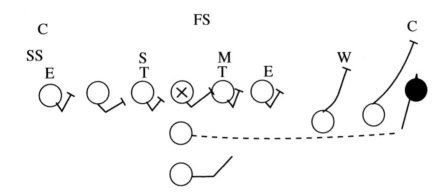

Blocking Rules:

Playside tackle —	Block 2400/2500.
Playside guard —	Block 2400/2500.
Center —	Block 2400/2500.
Backside guard —	Block 2400/2500.
Backside tackle —	Block 2400/2500.
Tight end —	Block 2400/2500.

Backfield Coaching Points:

Z —	Block the number 1 defender.
X —	Jab step; catch ball behind LOS.
FB —	Block the number 2 defender.
TB —	Fake 24/25.
QB —	Open one step; show ball for 24/25; deliver ball on second step to the X.

CHAPTER 3

OUTSIDE ZONE RUNNING PLAYS

INTRODUCTION TO OUTSIDE ZONE PLAYS TO THE SPLIT-END SIDE

The plays presented in this section of this chapter are designed to provide teams with the ability to get the ball to the perimeter on the split-end side. Over the years, our teams have averaged almost eight yards a carry on outside zone plays to the split-end side.

SPLIT END STRETCH BLOCKING RULES 28/29 SE

Playside tackle — Covered: reach; uncovered: "backer adjust"; maintain angle integrity; rip or punch and grab; deeper bucket step vs. loose or wide alignment.

Playside guard — Covered: reach; uncovered: 3-step bucket first-to-second level, maintain angle integrity on second level.

Center — Covered: reach; uncovered: 3-step bucket first-to-second level, maintain angle integrity on second level.

Backside guard — Covered: scoop; uncovered: scoop first-to-second level; chop all shades; stay high on 1 or 2 technique; chop all under. Backside tackle —Covered: scoop; uncovered: scoop; chop all 3 and 2 techniques; stay high on 4 technique.

Tight end — Scoop.

PLAY #41— "QUEEN RIGHT 28/29 SE SIDE"

4-3

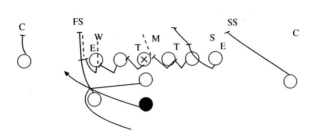

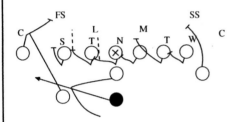

Reduced

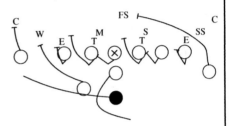

Slide Weak

Blocking Rules:

Playside tackle — Block 28/29 zone rules.

Playside guard — Block 28/29 zone rules.

Center — Block 28/29 zone rules.

Backside guard — Block 28/29 zone rules.

Backside tackle — Block 28/29 zone rules.

Tight end — Block 28/29 zone rules.

Backfield Coaching Points:

Z — Block the near safety; radical inside release.

X — Block man on; be aware of corner squeeze technique.

FB — Bongo; help with splitside tackle; block outside half of force defender.

TB — Open step one-yard deep and three yards outside of ghost TE's alignment; stay on course till something crosses your path, then make a north/south cut.

QB — Open at 10:00; spring ball to TB; continue on naked path.

PLAY #42 — "QUEEN RIGHT Z LIZ 28/29 SEAL SE"

4-3

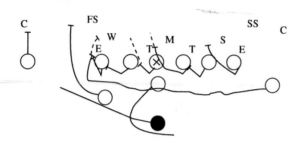

Reduced

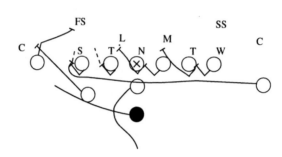

Slide Weak

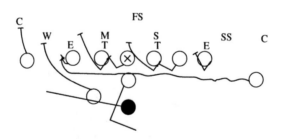

Blocking Rules:

Playside tackle — Block 28/29 zone rules.

Playside guard — Block 28/29 zone rules.

Center — Block 28/29 zone rules.

Backside guard — Block 28/29 zone rules.

Backside tackle — Block 28/29 zone rules.

Tight end — Block 28/29 zone rules.

Backfield Coaching Points:

Z — Motion across formation to help tackle seal EMOL.

X — 28/29 rules.

FB — No help needed for split tackle; block outside half of force defender.

TB — Run 28/29.

QB — Run 28/29.

PLAY # 43 — "QUEEN RIGHT TWINS 28/29 SE"

4-3

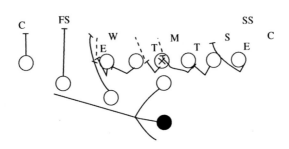

Reduced

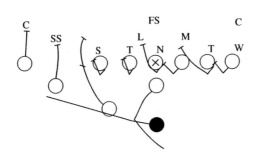

Slide Weak

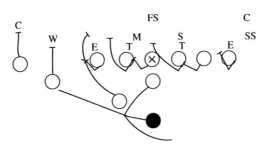

Blocking Rules:

Playside tackle — Block 28/29 zone rules.

Playside guard — Block 28/29 zone rules.

Center — Block 28/29 zone rules.

Backside guard — Block 28/29 zone rules.

Backside tackle — Block 28/29 zone rules.

Tight end — Block 28/29 zone rules.

Backfield Coaching Points:

Z — Block the #2 defender.

X — Block man on.

FB — Bongo with splitside tackle, looking inside for first wrong colored jersey.

TB — Run 28/29.

QB — Run 28/29.

PLAY # 44 —"QUEEN RIGHT TWINS 28/29 DOUBLE CRACK SE SIDE"

4-3

Reduced

Slide Weak

Blocking Rules:

Playside tackle — Block 28/29 zone rules.

Playside guard — Block 28/29 zone rules.

Center — Block 28/29 zone rules.

Backside guard — Block 28/29 zone rules.

Backside tackle — Block 28/29 zone rules.

Tight end — Block 28/29 zone rules.

Backfield Coaching Points:

Z — Crack on the first defender on second level aligned inside of you.

X — Crack on first defender on second or third level aligned inside of you.

FB — Block the defender responsible for outside third of coverage or any rolled corner look.

TB — Run 28/29.

QB — Run 28/29.

4-3

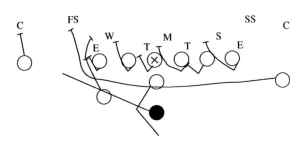

Reduced

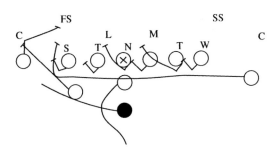

Slide Weak

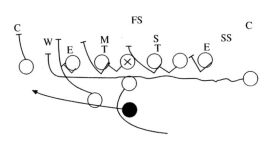

Blocking Rules:

Playside tackle — Block 28/29 zone rules.

Playside guard — Block 28/29 zone rules.

Center — Block 28/29 zone rules.

Backside guard — Block 28/29 zone rules.

Backside tackle — Block 28/29 zone rules.

Tight end — Block 28/29 zone rules.

Backfield Coaching Points:

Z — Run motion across formation; block the outside half of defender responsible for force.

X — Block man.

FB — Bongo with splitside tackle, looking for first wrong colored jersey.

TB — Run 28/29.

QB — Run 28/29.

PLAY #46 — "QUEEN RIGHT 28/29 CRACK SE"

4-3

Reduced

Slide Weak

Blocking Rules:

Playside tackle— Block 28/29 zone rules.

Playside guard — Block 28/29 zone rules.

Center — Block 28/29 zone rules.

Backside guard — Block 28/29 zone rules.

Backside tackle — Block 28/29 zone rules.

Tight end — Block 28/29 zone rules.

Backfield Coaching Points:

Z — Block the near safety.

X — Crack block on the defender responsible for force.

FB — Exchange responsibilities with X and block the defender responsible for outside third; if rolled, corner block him.

TB — Run 28/29.

QB — Run 28/29.

PLAY # 47 — "TRIPS RIGHT 28/29 EDGE SE"

4-3

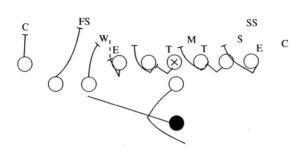

Reduced

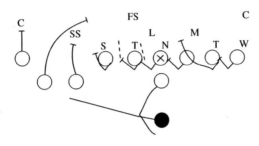

Slide Weak

Blocking Rules:

Playside tackle — Block 28/29 zone rules.

Playside guard — Block 28/29 zone rules.

Center — Block 28/29 zone rules.

Backside guard — Block 28/29 zone rules.

Backside tackle — Bock 28/29 zone rules.

Tight end — Block 28/29 zone rules.

Backfield Coaching Points:

Z — Block the #2 defender.

X — Block man on.

FB — Block the defender responsible for force.

TB — Run 28/29.

QB — Run 28/29.

PLAY # 48 — "DEUCE RIGHT 28/29 EDGE SE SIDE"

4-3

Reduced

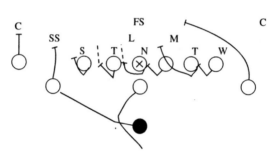

Slide Weak

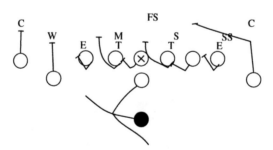

Blocking Rules:

Playside tackle — Block 28/29 zone rules.

Playside guard — Block 28/29 zone rules.

Center — Block 28/29 zone rules.

Backside guard — Block 28/29 zone rules.

Backside tackle — Block 28/29 zone rules.

Tight end — Block 28/29 zone rules.

Backfield Coaching Points:

Z — Block the near safety.

X — Block man on.

FB — Block outside half of defender responsible for force.

TB — Run 28/29.

QB — Run 28/29.

PLAY #49 — "DUO RIGHT F LIZ 28/29 SE SIDE"

4-3

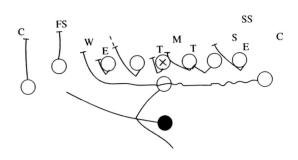

Reduced

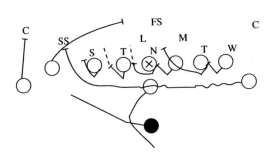

Slide Weak

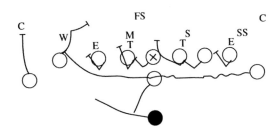

Blocking Rules:

Playside tackle — Block 28/29 zone rules.

Playside guard — Block 28/29 zone rules.

Center — Block 28/29 zone rules.

Backside guard — Block 28/29 zone rules.

Backside tackle — Block 28/29 zone rules.

Tight end — Block 28/29 zone rules.

Backfield Coaching Points:

Z — Block the near safety.

X — Block man on.

FB — Motion across formation; block outside half of force defender.

TB — Run 28/29.

QB — Run 28/29.

PLAY # 50 — "TREY RIGHT H LIZ 28/29 SMASH SE SIDE"

4-3

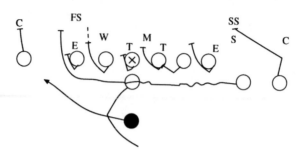

Reduced

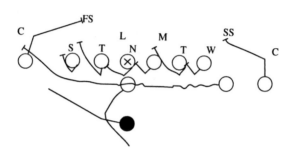

Slide Weak

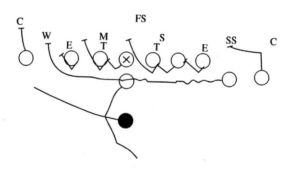

Blocking Rules:

Playside tackle — Block 28/29 zone rules.

Playside guard — Block 28/29 zone rules.

Center — Block 28/29 zone rules.

Backside guard — Block 28/29 zone rules.

Backside tackle — Block 28/29 zone rules.

Tight end — Block 28/29 zone rules.

Backfield Coaching Points:

Z — Block the near safety.

X — Man on.

FB — Motion across formation; block outside half of defender.

TB — Run 28/29.

QB — Run 28/29.

PLAY # 51 — "TREY RIGHT H LIZ 28/29 SEAL"

4-3

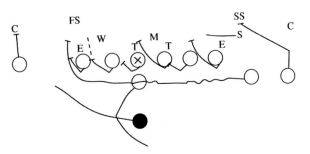

Reduced

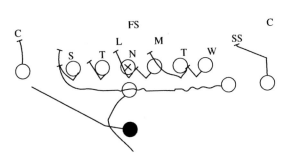

Slide Weak

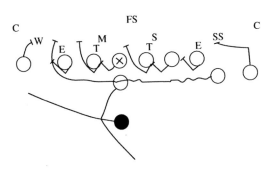

Blocking Rules:

Playside tackle — Block 28/29 zone rules.

Playside guard — Block 28/29 zone rules.

Center — Block 28/29 zone rules.

Backside guard — Block 28/29 zone rules.

Backside tackle — Block 28/29 zone rules.

Tight end — Block 28/29 zone rules.

Backfield Coaching Points:

Z — Block the near safety.

X — Block man on.

FB — Motion across formation; seal man on splitside tackle.

TB — Run 28/29.

QB — Run 28/29.

PLAY # 52 — "QUEEN RIGHT Z LEE 28/29 LEAD SE SIDE"

4-3

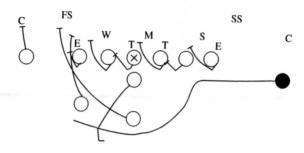

Reduced

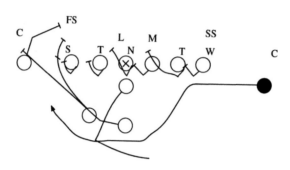

Slide Weak

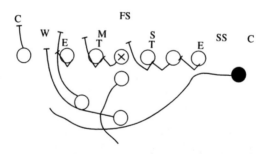

Blocking Rules:

Playside tackle — Block 28/29 zone rules.

Playside guard — Block 28/29 zone rules.

Center — Block 28/29 zone rules.

Backside guard — Block 28/29 zone rules.

Backside tackle — Block 28/29 zone rules.

Tight end — Block 28/29 zone rules.

Backfield Coaching Points:

Z — Orbit motion; receive ball from QB; run 28/29.

X — Block man on.

FB — Bongo with splitside tackle; work upfield looking inside for first wrong colored jersey.

TB — Block outside half of force defender.

QB — Run 28/29.

INTRODUCTION TO THE OUSIDE ZONE PLAYS TO THE TIGHT-END SIDE

Outside zone plays to the tight-end side are among the most difficult plays to execute in the zone offense. The type of force that the defense gives a team makes it essential that the team varies its attack to the tight-end side. The plays included in this section of this chapter offer a team a multiplicity of ways to attack the perimeter to its tight-end side.

TIGHT END STRETCH BLOCKING RULES 28/29 TE

Playside tackle — Covered: reach; uncovered: 3-step bucket progression.

Playside guard — Covered: read; uncovered: 3-step bucket progression — first-to- second level.

Center — Covered: read; uncovered: 3-step bucket — first-to-second level.

Backside guard — Covered: scoop; uncovered: scoop first-to-second level.

Backside tackle — Covered: scoop; uncovered: chop all 3 and 2 techniques; stay high on the 4 technique or slant.

Tight end — Covered: read the 7 technique; get movement upfield; drop and pop; eyes to inside linebacker.

PLAY #53 — "KING RIGHT 28/29 TE SIDE"

4-3

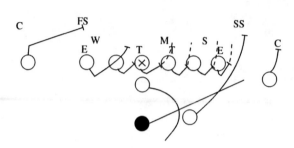

Reduced

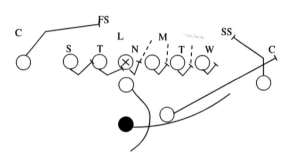

Slide Weak

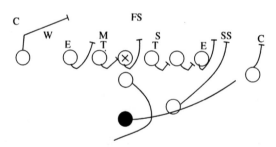

Blocking Rules:

Playside tackle — Block 28/29 zone rules

Playside guard — Block 28/29 zone rules.

Center — Block 28/29 zone rules.

Backside guard — Block 28/29 zone rules.

Backside tackle — Block 28/29 zone rules.

Tight end — Block 28/29 zone rules.

Backfield Coaching Points:

Z — Block man on.

X — Block the near safety.

FB — Responsible for the force of the defense.

TB — Open step one yard deep and three yards outside of TE's alignment; stay on course.

QB — Open at 10:00; sprint the ball to the TB; run a naked course.

4-3

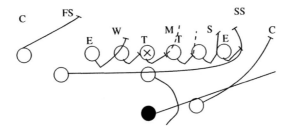

Reduced

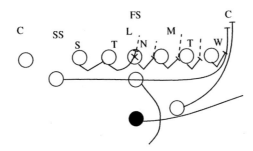

Slide Weak

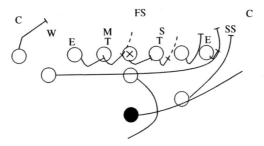

Blocking Rules:

Playside tackle — Block 28/29 zone rules.

Playside guard — Block 28/29 zone rules.

Center — Block 28/29 zone rules.

Backside guard — Block 28/29 zone rules.

Backside tackle — Block 28/29 zone rules.

Tight end — Block 28/29 zone rules.

Backfield Coaching Points:

Z — Motion across the formation; seal the block the man on the TE.

X — Block the near safety.

FB — Responsible for the force of the defense.

TB — Run 28/29.

QB — Run 28/29.

PLAY # 55 — "KING RIGHT TWINS Z RIP 28/29 SMASH TE"

4-3

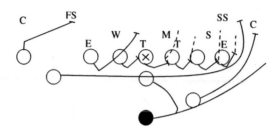

Reduced

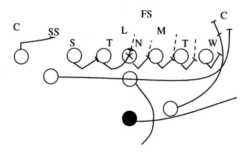

Slide Weak

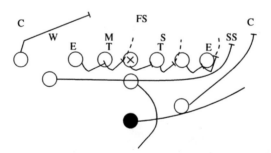

Blocking Rules:

Playside tackle — Block 28/29 zone rules.

Playside guard — Block 28/29 zone rules.

Center — Block 28/29 zone rules.

Backside guard — Block 28/29 zone rules.

Backside tackle — Block 28/29 zone rules.

Tight end — Block 28/29 zone rules.

Backfield Coaching Points:

Z — Motion across the formation; block the force of the defense.

X — Block the near safety.

FB — Help TE on EMOL; work upfield, looking inside from second-to-third level.

TB — Run 28/29.

QB — Run 28/29.

4-3

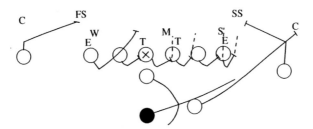

Reduced

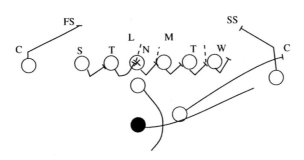

Slide Weak

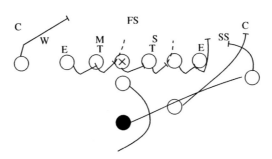

Blocking Rules:

Playside tackle — Block 28/29 zone rules.

Playside guard — Block 28/29 zone rules.

Center — Block 28/29 zone rules.

Backside guard — Block 28/29 zone rules.

Backside tackle — Block 28/29 zone rules.

Tight end — Block 28/29 zone rules.

Backfield Coaching Points:

Z — Crack block on the force defender.

X — Block the near safety.

FB — Exchange responsibilities with the Z receiver.

TB — Run 28/29

QB — Run 28/29.

57 — "KING RIGHT TWINS Z RAY 28/29 LEAD TE"

4-3

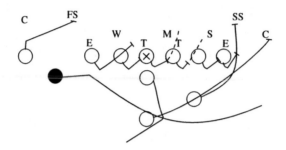

Reduced

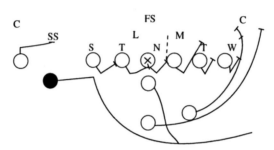

Slide Weak

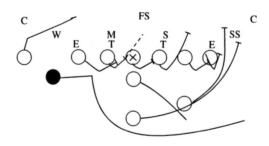

Blocking Rules:

Playside tackle — Block 28/29 zone rules.

Playside ggard — Block 28/29 zone rules.

Center — Block 28/29 zone rules.

Backside guard — Block 28/29 zone rules.

Backside tackle — Block 28/29 zone rules.

Tight end — Block 28/29 zone rules.

Backfield Coaching Points:

Z — Orbit motion; receive ball from the QB; run 28/29.

X — Block the near safety.

FB — Run a seal block with TE, looking inside second-to-third level.

TB — Block the force of the defender.

QB — Run 28/29.

4-3

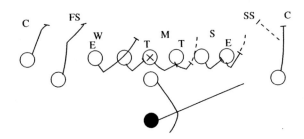

Reduced

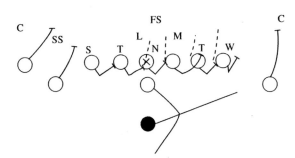

Slide Weak

Blocking Rules:

Playside tackle — Block 28/29 zone rules.

Playside guard — Block 28/29 zone rules.

Center — Block 28/29 zone rules.

Backside guard — Block 28/29 zone rules.

Backside tackle — Block 28/29 zone rules.

Tight end — Block 28/29 zone rules.

Backfield Coaching Points:

Z — Block man on.

X — Block the near safety.

Mustang — Responsible for the force of the defense.

TB — Run 28/29.

QB — Run 28/29.

PLAY # 59 — "DUO RIGHT 28/29 EDGE TE"

4-3

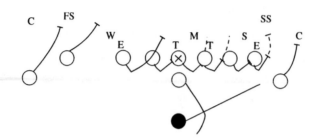

Reduced

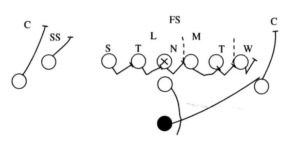

Slide Weak

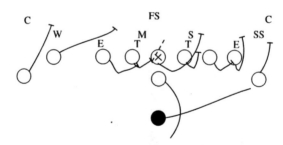

Blocking Rules:

Playside tackle — Block 28/29 zone rules.

Playside guard — Block 28/29 zone rules.

Center — Block 28/29 zone rules.

Backside guard — Block 28/29 zone rules.

Backside tackle — Block 28/29 zone rules.

Tight end — Block 28/29 zone rules.

Backfield Coaching Points:

Z — Block the near safety.

X — Inside release; block first wrong colored jersey that crosses your face.

FB — From wing position, block outside half of defender responsible for force.

TB — Run 28/29.

QB — Run 28/29.

PLAY # 60 — "DEUCE RIGHT H RIP 28/29 EDGE TE SIDE"

4-3

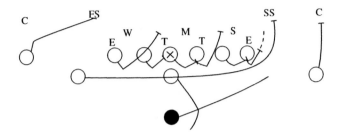

Reduced

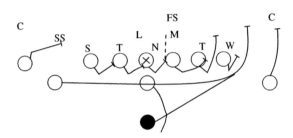

Slide Weak

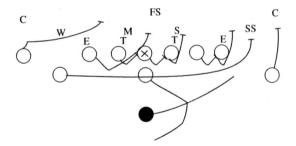

Blocking Rules:

Playside tackle — Block 28/29 zone rules.

Playside guard — Block 28/29 zone rules.

Center — Block 28/29 zone rules.

Backside guard — Block 28/29 zone rules.

Backside tackle — Block 28/29 zone rules.

Tight end — Block 28/29 zone rules.

Backfield Coaching Points:

Z — Block man on.

X — Block the near safety.

FB — Motion across formation; block the force defender.

TB — Run 28/29.

QB — Run 28/29.

PLAY # 61 — "DUO RIGHT F RETURN 28/29 EDGE TE"

4-3

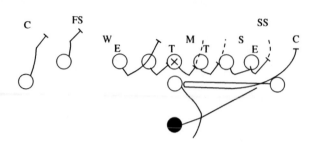

Reduced

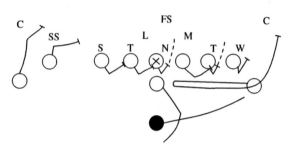

Slide Weak

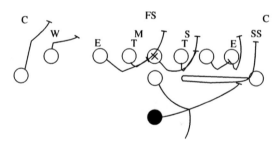

Blocking Rules:

Playside tackle —	Block 28/29 zone rules.
Playside guard —	Block 28/29 zone rules.
Center —	Block 28/29 zone rules.
Backside guard —	Block 28/29 zone rules.
Backside tackle —	Block 28/29 zone rules.
Tight end —	Block 28/29 zone rules.

Backfield Coaching Points:

Z —	Block the near safety.
X —	Release inside; block the first wrong colored jersey to cross your face.
FB —	From wing position, motion by the center; return to your original position; block the force defender.
TB —	Run 28/29.
QB —	Run 28/29.

CHAPTER 4

OUTSIDE ZONE PLAY-ACTION PASS PLAYS

PLAY #62 — "KING RIGHT 2800/2900 TE"

4-3

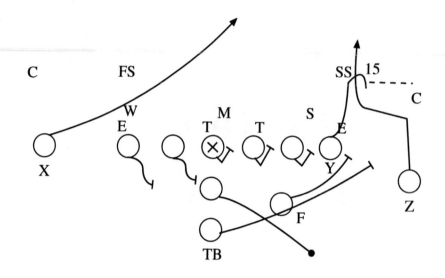

Blocking Rules:

Playside tackle — Block 28/29.

Playside guard — Block 28/29.

Center — Block 28/29.

Backside guard — Modify your pass drop.

Backside tackle — Modify your pass drop.

Tight end — 15-yard read route.

Backfield Coaching Points:

Z — Run a crack go route.

X — Run a climb post route.

FB — Fake 28/29; block C gap.

TB — Fake 28/29; block C-to-D gap.

QB — Fake 28/29; then set up outside of PST's alignment.

PLAY #63 — "KING RIGHT 2800/2900 SAIL TE"

4-3

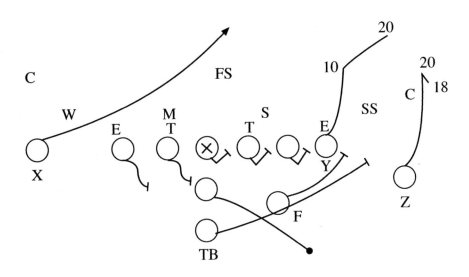

Blocking Rules:

Playside tackle — Block 28/29.

Playside guard — Block 28/29.

Center — Block 28/29.

Backside guard — Modify your pass set.

Backside tackle — Modify your pass set.

Tight end — Run a sail route.

Backfield Coaching Points:

Z — Run a deep comeback out route at 20-to-18 yards.

X — Run a climb post route.

FB — Fake 28/29; block C gap.

TB — Fake 28/29; block C-to-D gap.

QB — Fake 28/29; then set up outside of PST's alignment.

PLAY #64 — "DEUCE RIGHT 2800/2900 TE"

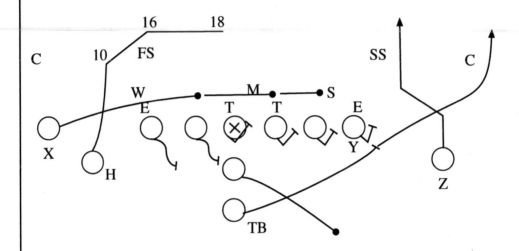

Blocking Rules:

Playside tackle — Run 28/29.

Playside guard — Run 28/29.

Center — Run 28/29.

Backside guard — Modify your pass set.

Backside tackle — Modify your pass set.

Tight end — Run 28/29.

Backfield Coaching Points:

Z — Run a crack go route.

X — Run a post-dig route at 16-18 yards.

FB — Run a dart route no deeper than six yards; find the hole.

TB — Fake 28/29; check D gap; if there is no rusher, run a wheel route.

QB — Fake 28/29; then set up outside of PST's alignment.

PLAY # 65 — "QUEEN RIGHT 2900/2800 SE"

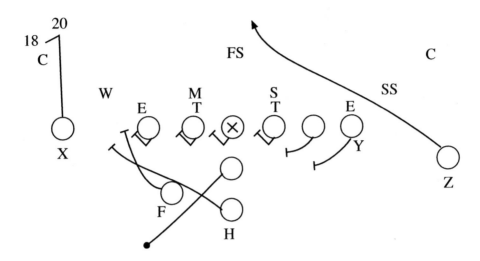

Blocking Rules:

Playside tackle — Run 28/29.

Playside guard — Run 28/29.

Center — Run 28/29.

Backside guard — Run 28/29.

Backside tackle — Modify your pass set.

Tight end — Modify your pass set.

Backfield Coaching Points:

Z — Run a climb post route.

X — Run a deep comeback out at 20-to- 18 yards.

FB — Fake 28/29; block C gap.

TB — Fake 28/29; block C-to-D gap.

QB — Fake 28/29; then set up outside of PST's alignment.

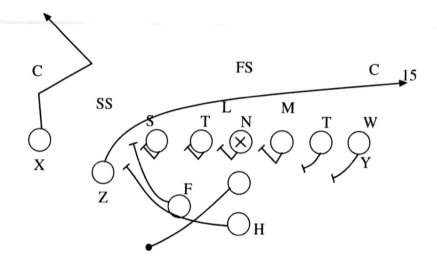

Blocking Rules:

Playside tackle — Run 28/29.

Playside guard — Run 28/29.

Center — Run 28/29.

Backside guard — Run 28/29.

Backside tackle — Modify your pass set.

Tight end — Modify your pass set.

Backfield Coaching Points:

Z — Run a crossing route, working shallow to deep.

X — Run a post corner.

FB — Fake 28/29; block C gap.

TB — Fake 28/29; block C-to-D gap.

QB — Fake 28/29.

PLAY #67 — "QUEEN RIGHT 28/29 NAKED SE"

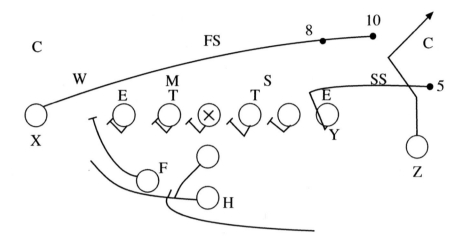

Blocking Rules:

Playside tackle — Run 28/29.

Playside guard — Run 28/29.

Center — Run 28/29.

Backside guard — Run 28/29.

Backside tackle — Run 28/29.

Tight end — Stop as in 28/29; then run a flat route to a depth of five yards.

Backfield Coaching Points:

Z — Run a post-corner route.

X — Run a crossing route from 8-10 yards; sit vs. zone; keep on move vs. man.

FB — Fake 28/29.

TB — Fake 28/29.

QB — Fake 28/29; run naked course; read high to low.

PLAY #68 — "TRIPS RIGHT 29 NAKED OVER"

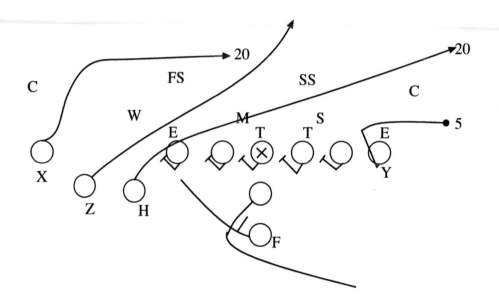

Blocking Rules:

Playside tackle — Run 28/29.

Playside guard — Run 28/29.

Center — Run 28/29.

Backside guard — Run 28/29.

Backside tackle — Run 28/29.

Tight end — Fake 28/29; run flat route.

Backfield Coaching Points:

Z — Run a climb post.

X — Run a come open late.

Mustang — Run over route to a depth of 20 yards.

TB — Fake 28/29.

QB — Fake 28/29; run naked course; read high to low.

CHAPTER 5

OPTION PLAYS

INTRODUCTION TO OPTION SERIES PLAYS

The option plays presented in this chapter provide a team with a way to attack defenses without changing its basic zone-blocking schemes. Both the inside and the outside options give a team the ability to force the defense to remove defenders from the box.

4-3

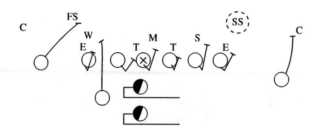

Reduced

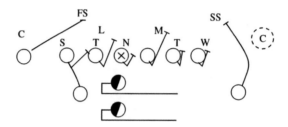

Slide Weak

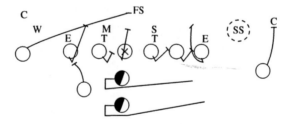

Blocking Rules:

Playside tackle — Block 24/25 zone.

Playside guard — Block 24/25 zone.

Center — Block 24/25 zone.

Backside guard — Block 24/25 zone.

Backside tackle — Block 24/25 zone.

Tight end — Block 24/25 zone.

Backfield Coaching Points:

Z — Do not block primary run support.

X — Block the near safety.

FB — Under or man it call.

TB — Whirly bird option path.

QB — Whirly bird option course; option force.

PLAY #70 — "14/15 G TE SIDE"

4-3

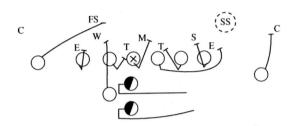

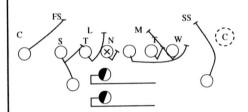

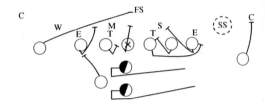

Reduced   Slide Weak

Blocking Rules:

Playside tackle — Uncovered: block down and fill for guard; covered:combo with TE.

Playside guard — Pull and log or kick out EMOL.

Center —   Covered: frontside A gap; uncovered: vs. slide weak combowith backside guard to second level.

Backside guard —Weakside: A, if threat; no threat: weak A combo with center to second level.

Backside tackle —Inside zone rules.

Tight end —   Tackle covered: combo;tackle uncovered: first, second-level player inside.

Backfield Coaching Points:

Z —   Do not block primary run support (force).

X —   Block the near safety.

FB —   Block 24/25.

TB —   Whirly bird option path.

QB —   Whirly bird option course; option force.

4-3

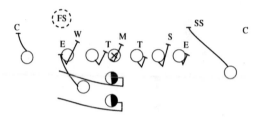

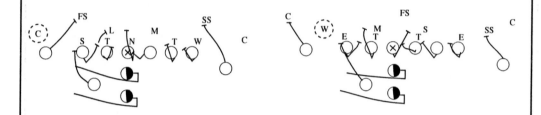

Reduced   Slide Weak

Blocking Rules:

Playside tackle — 3 technique on the guard; combo to the second level; anything else, cut off the first linebacker on the second level.

Playside guard — 3 technique combo with the tackle; anything else, block man; uncovered: combo with the center.

Center — Frontside: shade block down; anything else, combo with the playside guard.

Backside guard — Uncovered: work with the center scoop to second level; covered: tighten landmark; work vertically.

Backside tackle — Uncovered: scoop with the backside guard.

Tight end — Block man on; tight on landmark; work vertically.

Backfield Coaching Points:

Z — Near safety.

X — Cover 8 — corner; cover 2 — FS, Cover 3 — corner; cover 1-4 — run off.

FB — Load block on EMOL.

TB — Whirly bird option path.

QB — Whirly bird option course; option force.

PLAY #72 — "14/15 Z REVERSE"

4-3

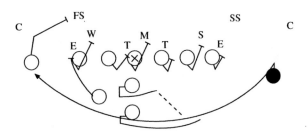

Reduced

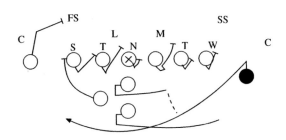

Slide Weak

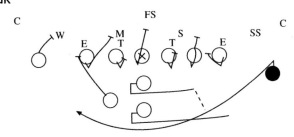

Blocking Rules:

Playside tackle — Block 24/25 zone.

Playside guard — Block 24/25 zone.

Center — Block 24/25 zone.

Backside guard — Block 24/25 zone.

Backside tackle — Block 24/25 zone.

Tight end — Block 24/25 zone.

Backfield Coaching Points:

Z — Jab step; run reverse course.

X — Stalk off; crack near safety; except vs. slide weak; block the Will.

FB — Pin end man on LOS.

TB — Whirly bird; deepen option path.

QB — Whirly bird; pitch the ball to Z on reverse path.

PLAY #73 — "14/15 OPEN X REVERSE"

4-3

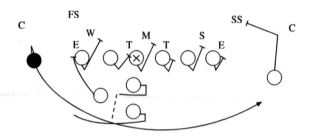

Reduced

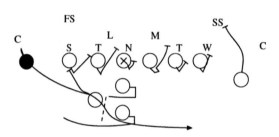

Slide Weak

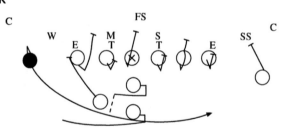

Blocking Rules:

Playside tackle — Block 14/15 open.

Playside guard — Block 14/15 open.

Center — Block 14/15 open.

Backside guard — Block 14/15 open.

Backside tackle — Block 14/15 open.

Tight end — Block 14/15 open; try to pin end man on LOS.

Backfield Coaching Points:

Z — Stalk off; crack near safety; except vs. slide weak, then crack strong safety.

X — Jab step; run reverse course.

FB — Block 14/15 open.

TB — Whirly bird; deepen option path.

QB — Whirly bird; pitch the ball to X on reverse path.

PLAY #74 — "18/19 TE"

4-3

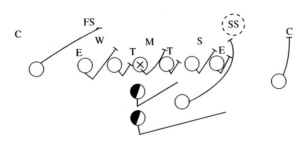

Reduced

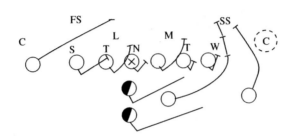

Slide Weak

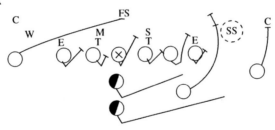

Blocking Rules:

Playside tackle — Block 28/29.

Playside guard — Block 28/29.

Center — Block 28/29.

Backside guard — Block 28/29.

Backside tackle — Block 28/29.

Tight end — Block 28/29.

Backfield Coaching Points:

Z — Do not block primary run support.

X — Near safety.

FB — Bongo with TE, looking inside second-to-third level.

TB — Drop step; pitch phase with QB.

QB — Kick back the opposite foot of play; attack the edge downhill; option off of the force.

4-3

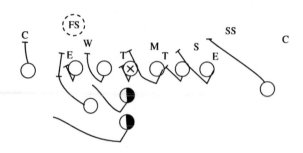

Reduced

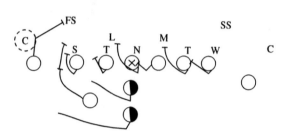

Slide Weak

Blocking Rules:

Playside tackle — Block 28/29.

Playside guard — Block 28/29.

Center — Block 28/29.

Backside guard — Block 28/29.

Backside tackle — Block 28/29.

Tight end — Block 28/29.

Backfield Coaching Points:

Z — Near safety.

X — Do not block primary run support.

FB — Bongo with splitside tackle second-to-third level.

TB — Drop step; pitch phase with QB.

QB — Kick back the opposite foot of play; attack the edge downhill; option off of the force.

PLAY #76 — "18/19 STICK TE SIDE"

4-3

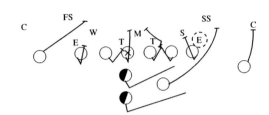

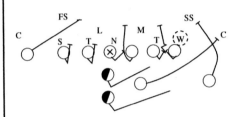

| Reduced | Slide Weak |

Blocking Rules:

Playside tackle — Uncovered: combo with guard; covered: combo with TE.

Playside guard — Uncovered: combo with center; covered: combo with tackle.

Center — Covered: combo playside; uncovered: combo backside.

Backside guard — Weak shade: combo with center; covered: tighten landmark; base block.

Backside tackle — Block man on; tighter landmark.

Tight end — Tackle covered: combo; tackle uncovered: second level; vs. slide weak, outside release block the FS.

Backfield Coaching Points:

Z — Man responsible for outside third; cover 2, stay on corner.

X — Near safety.

FB — Block force.

TB — Drop step; option course.

QB — Opposite foot drop; option EMOL; be prepared to pitch.

PLAY #77 — "18/19 STICK SE SIDE"

4-3

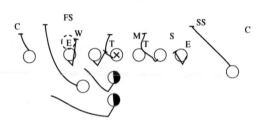

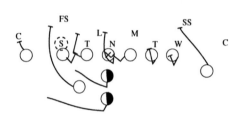

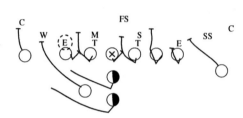

Reduced   Slide Weak

Blocking Rules:

Playside tackle — Guard covered: combo with guard; guard uncovered: work to second level.

Playside guard — Covered: combo with tackle; uncovered: combo with center.

Center — Playside shade: combo with center; backside shade: combo with backside guard.

Backside guard — Uncovered: combo with center; covered: tighten landmark; base man on.

Backside tackle — Uncovered: combo with guard; covered: tighten landmark; base man on.

Tight end — Base man on; tighten landmark.

Backfield Coaching Points:

Z — Near safety.

X — Block outside third rolled corner in cover 2.

FB — Block force.

TB — Drop step option phase.

QB — Drop opposite foot; option end man on LOS; be prepared to pitch.

PLAY #78 — "18/19 Z REVERSE"

4-3

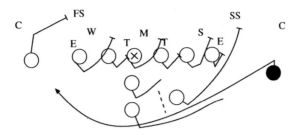

Reduced

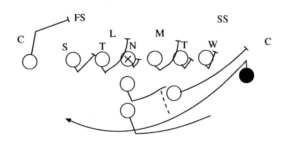

Slide Weak

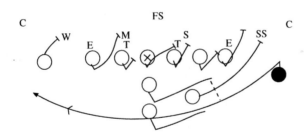

Blocking Rules:

Playside tackle — Block 28/29.

Playside guard — Block 28/29.

Center — Block 28/29.

Backside guard — Block 28/29.

Backside tackle — Start 28/29 path; then circle around to pick off the defender chasing the reverse.

Tight end — Block 28/29.

Backfield Coaching Points:

Z — Jab step; then come back on path to take the pitch from the QB.

X — Near safety vs. slide weak, be prepared to crack on Will.

FB — Block force.

TB — Drop step; deepen path; carry out fake.

QB — Opposite foot drop; pitch the ball to Z.

4-3

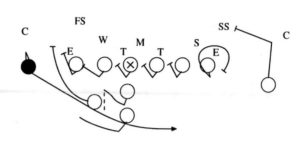

Reduced

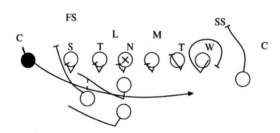

Slide Weak

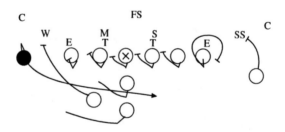

Blocking Rules:

Playside tackle — Block 28/29.

Playside guard — Block 28/29.

Center — Block 28/29.

Backside guard — Block 28/29.

Backside tackle — Block 28/29.

Tight end — Start to block 28/29; circle the wagon around; pick off any defender charging.

Backfield Coaching Points:

Z — Block the near safety.

X — Jab step; path back to receive pitch from QB.

FB — Block force.

TB — Drop step; deepen path.

QB — Drop opposite foot; pitch the ball to X.

PLAY #80 — "18/19 Z REVERSE PASS"

4-3

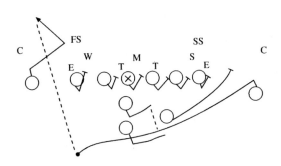

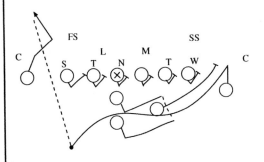

Reduced

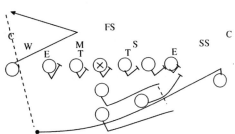

Slide Weak

Blocking Rules:

Playside tackle — Block 28/29.

Playside guard — Block 28/29.

Center — Block 28/29.

Backside guard — Block 28/29.

Backside tackle — Block 28/29.

Tight end — Block 28/29.

Backfield Coaching Points:

Z — Jab step; sell reverse; hit X on crack corner.

X — Sell crack block on the near safety; bend corner route to outside third.

FB — Block force.

TB — Fake 18/19; block first wrong colored jersey.

QB — Drop opposite foot; pitch the ball to Z; block first wrong colored jersey.

PLAY #81 — "18/19 X REVERSE PASS"

4-3

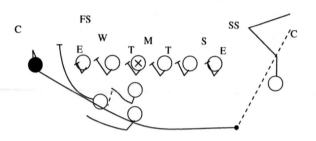

Reduced

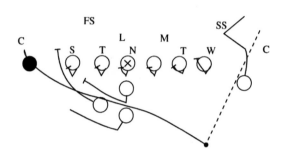

Slide Weak

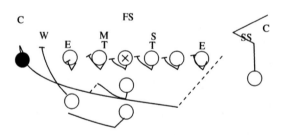

Blocking Rules:

Playside tackle — Block 28/29.

Playside guard — Block 28/29.

Center — Block 28/29.

Backside guard — Block 28/29.

Backside tackle — Block 28/29.

Tight end — Block 28/29.

Backfield Coaching Points:

Z — Sell crack; block on the near safety; run corner cut to outside third.

X — Jab step; take pitch; sell reverse throw to the corner.

FB — Block force.

TB — Fake 18/19 reverse; block first wrong colored jersey.

QB — Fake 18/19 reverse; block first wrong colored jersey.

PLAY #82 — "18/19 CRACK SE SIDE"

4-3

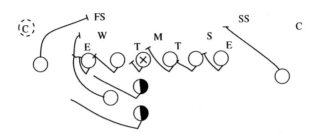

Reduced

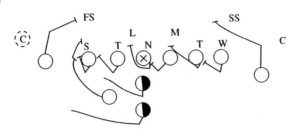

Slide Weak

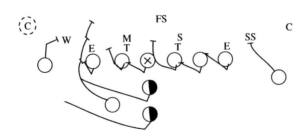

Blocking Rules:

Playside tackle — Block 28/29.

Playside guard — Block 28/29.

Center — Block 28/29.

Backside guard — Block 28/29.

Backside tackle — Block 28/29.

Tight end — Block 28/29.

Backfield Coaching Points:

Z — Block the near safety.

X — Crack on force; vs. cover 2, crack on the near half-field safety.

FB — Bongo with split tackle, looking inside second-to-third level.

TB — Drop step; pitch phase.

QB — Drop opposite foot; option secondary run support.

PLAY #83 — "18/19 CRACK TE SIDE"

4-3

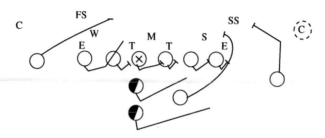

Reduced

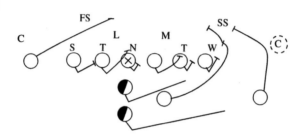

Slide Weak

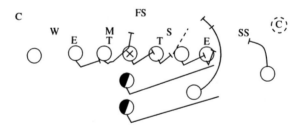

Blocking Rules:

Playside tackle — Block 28/29.

Playside guard — Block 28/29.

Center — Block 28/29.

Backside guard — Block 28/29.

Backside tackle — Block 28/29.

Tight end — Block 28/29.

Backfield Coaching Points:

Z — Crack on force of secondary coverage.

X — Block the near safety.

FB — Bongo with TE, looking inside second and third level.

TB — Drop step; option phase with QB.

QB — Drop step with opposite foot; option secondary run support.

PLAY #84 — "18/19 TWINS SE SIDE DOUBLE CRACK"

4-3

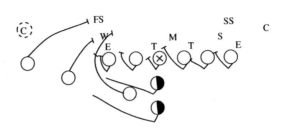

Reduced

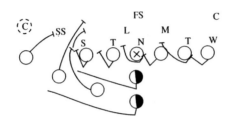

Slide Weak

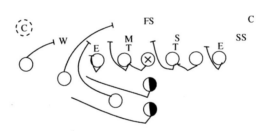

Blocking Rules:

Playside tackle — Block 28/29.

Playside guard — Block 28/29.

Center — Block 28/29.

Backside guard — Block 28/29.

Backside tackle — Block 28/29.

Tight end — Block 28/29.

Backfield Coaching Points:

Z — 3-linebacker set, crack on OLB; 2-linebacker set, read crack up to free.

X — 3-linebacker set, crack on near safety; 2-linebacker set, crack on force.

FB — Bongo with splitside tackler, looking inside second and third level.

TB — Drop step; option phase.

QB — Drop opposite foot; option secondary run support.

PLAY #85 — "18/19 TREY FORMATION DOUBLE CRACK"

4-3

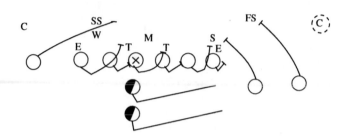

Reduced

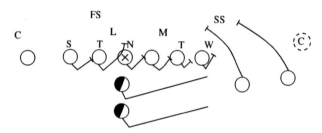

Slide Weak

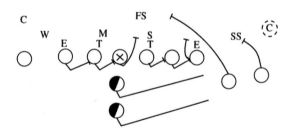

Blocking Rules:

Playside tackle — Block 28/29.

Playside guard — Block 28/29.

Center — Block 28/29.

Backside guard — Block 28/29.

Backside tackle — Block 28/29.

Tight end — Block 28/29.

Backfield Coaching Points:

Z — Crack on force.

X — Near safety.

FB — 3-linebakcer set, OLB; 2-linebacker set, work inside to the near safety.

TB — Drop step; option phase.

QB — Drop opposite foot; option secondary run support.

4-3

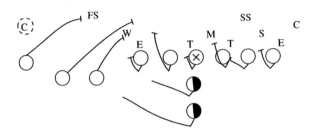

Reduced

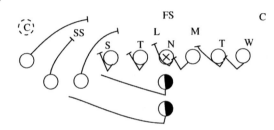

Slide Weak

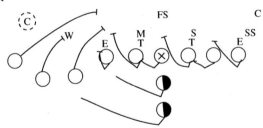

Blocking Rules:

Playside tackle — Block 28/29.

Playside guard — Block 28/29.

Center — Block 28/29.

Backside guard — Block 28/29.

Backside tackle — Block 28/29.

Tight end — Block 28/29.

Backfield Coaching Points:

Z — Crack on force.

X — Crack on middle-third or deep-half defender.

FB — Bongo, looking inside second-to-third level.

TB — Drop step; pitch phase with QB.

QB — Kick back opposite foot of play; attack the edge downhill; option off of the force.

PLAY #87 — "DUO RIGHT 14 G TE SIDE"

4-3

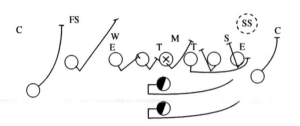

Reduced

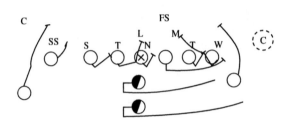

Slide Weak

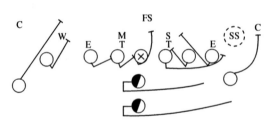

Blocking Rules:

Playside tackle — Covered: combo with TE; uncovered: combo with guard.

Playside guard — Pull and log or kick out EMOL.

Center — Covered: frontside A gap; uncovered: work backside combo.

Backside guard — Weakside A gap, if threat; no weak A, combo with center to second level.

Backside tackle — Block 24/25.

Tight end — Tackle covered: combo; tackle uncovered: first second-level player inside.

Backfield Coaching Points:

Z — Cut off the first wrong colored jersey.

X — Near safety.

FB — From wing position, do not block force; block secondary run support.

TB — Whirly bird option phase.

QB — Whirly bird option phase; option force.

PLAY # 88 — "DUO LEFT 19"

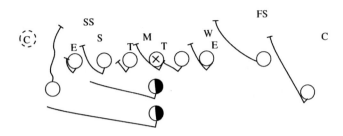

4-3

Reduced

Slide Weak

Blocking Rules:

Playside tackle — Block 28/29.

Playside guard — Block 28/29.

Center — Block 28/29.

Backside guard — Block 28/29.

Backside tackle — Block 28/29.

Tight end — Block 28/29.

Backfield Coaching Points:

Z — Inside release; block first wrong colored jersey.

X — Block the near safety.

FB — Bongo with TE, looking inside second and third level.

TB — Drop step; option phase.

QB — Drop opposite foot; option force.

PLAY # 89 — "KING RIGHT F LIZ 19"

4-3

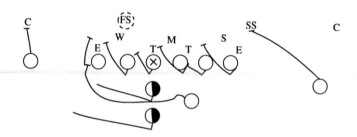

Reduced

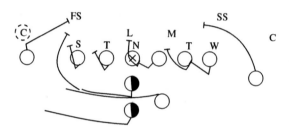

Slide Weak

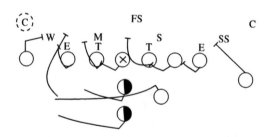

Blocking Rules:

Playside tackle — Block 28/29.

Playside guard — Block 28/29.

Center — Block 28/29.

Backside guard — Block 28/29.

Backside tackle — Block 28/29.

Tight end — Block 28/29.

Backfield Coaching Points:

Z — Block the near safety.

X — Do not block force.

FB — Bongo with splitside tackle, looking inside second and third level.

TB — Drop step; option phase.

QB — Drop opposite foot; option force of defense.

4-3

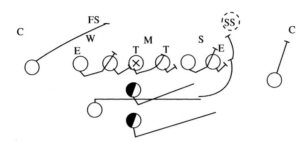

Reduced

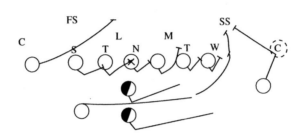

Slide Weak

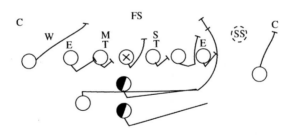

Blocking Rules:

Playside tackle — Block 28/29.

Playside guard — Block 28/29.

Center — Block 28/29.

Backside guard — Block 28/29.

Backside tackle — Block 28/29.

Tight end — Block 28/29.

Backfield Coaching Points:

Z — Do not block force.

X — Near safety.

FB — Bongo with TE, looking inside second-to-third level.

TB — Drop step; option phase.

QB — Drop opposite foot; option force.

PLAY #91 — "DEUCE RIGHT RIP 18 SEAL TE SIDE"

4-3

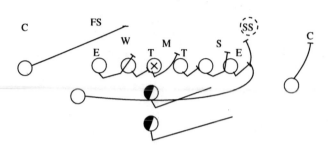

Reduced

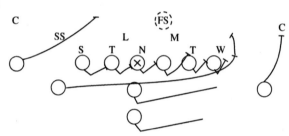

Slide Weak

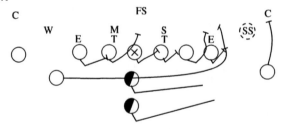

Blocking Rules:

Playside tackle — Block 28/29.

Playside guard — Block 28/29.

Center — Block 28/29.

Backside guard — Block 28/29.

Backside tackle — Block 28/29.

Tight end — Block 28/29.

Backfield Coaching Points:

Z — Do not block force.

X — Block the near safety.

FB — Seal block, looking inside second-to-third level.

TB — Drop step; option phase.

QB — Drop opposite foot; option force.

PLAY #92 — "TREY RIGHT H LIZ 19 SEAL SE SIDE"

4-3

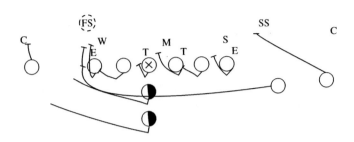

Reduced

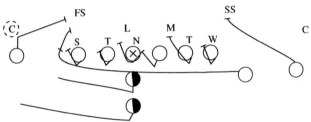

Slide Weak

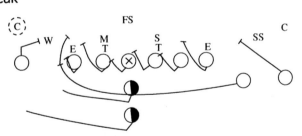

Blocking Rules:

Playside tackle — Block 28/29.

Playside guard — Block 28/29.

Center — Block 28/29.

Backside guard — Block 28/29.

Backside tackle — Block 28/29.

Tight end — Block 28/29.

Backfield Coaching Points:

Z — Near safety.

X — Do not block force.

FB — Seal block with split tackle, looking inside second-to-third level.

TB — Drop step; option phase.

QB — Drop opposite foot; option force.

PLAY #93 — "ACE 14 G"

4-3

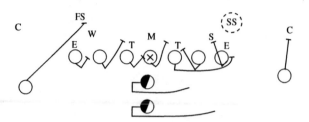

Reduced

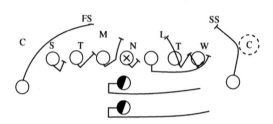

Slide Weak

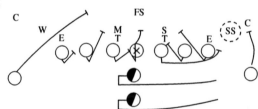

Blocking Rules:

Playside tackle — Uncovered: block down; covered: combo with TE.

Playside guard — Pull and log or kick out EMOL.

Center — Covered: frontside A gap; uncovered: vs. slide weak, combo with BSG.

Backside guard — Weakside A gap, if threat; no weak A, combo with center.

Backside tackle — Block 24/25.

Tight end — Tackle covered: combo; tackle uncovered: first second-level player inside.

Backfield Coaching Points:

Z — Do not block force.

X — Near safety.

FB — Block 24/25.

TB — Whirly bird; option phase.

QB — Whirly bird; option force.

CHAPTER 6

OPTION PLAY-ACTION PASS PLAYS

PLAY #94 — "QUEEN RIGHT 14 G PASS"

4-3

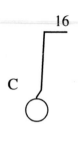
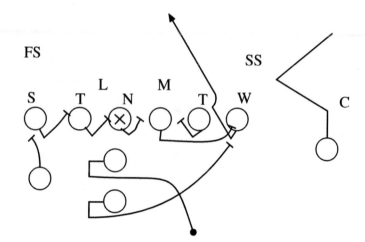

Blocking Rules:

Playside tackle —	14 G run rules.
Playside guard —	Pull and log or kick out EMOL.
Center —	Protect playside A gap.
Backside guard —	Protect backside A gap.
Backside tackle —	Protect backside B gap.
Tight end —	Inside release; run centerfield, looking to avoid contact.

Backfield Coaching Points:

Z —	Stalk crack corner route.
X —	Come open late at 16 yards.
FB —	Protect backside C gap.
TB —	Whirly bird option; attack any wrong colored jersey outside of pulling guard.
QB —	Whirly bird option; three steps; 5-step set up behind playside tackle's alignment.

PLAY #95 — "QUEEN LEFT TWINS 14 OPEN PASS"

4-3

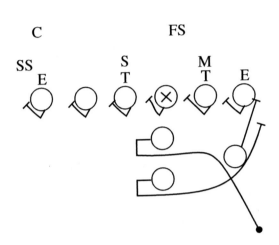
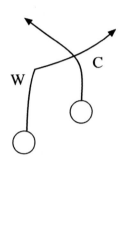

Blocking Rules:

Playside tackle —	Slide gap protection to the left (Lion call).
Playside guard —	Slide gap protection to the left (Lion call).
Center —	Slide gap protection to the left (Lion call).
Backside guard —	Slide gap protection to the left (Lion call).
Backside tackle —	Slide gap protection to the left (Lion call).
Tight end —	Slide gap protection to the left (Lion call).

Backfield Coaching Points:

Z —	Run a scissors cut off of X's inside break.
X —	Run a skinny post at 12-14 yards.
FB —	Block the C gap.
TB —	Whirly bird option; then attack C gap to D gap.
QB —	Whirly bird option; fake three steps; 5-step drop behind playside tackle's alignment.

PLAY #96 — "KING RIGHT 18 PASS"

4-3

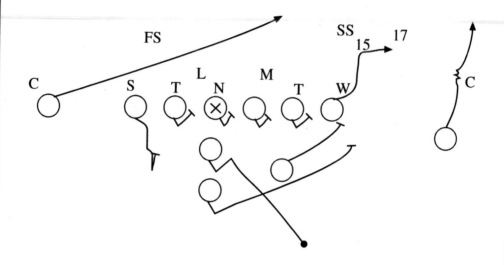

Blocking Rules:

Playside tackle —	Block 28/29.
Playside guard —	Block 28/29.
Center —	Block 28/29.
Backside guard —	Block 28/29.
Backside tackle —	Modify your 28/29 to a pass set drop.
Tight end —	Slam man on; run a bend route at 15-17 yards.

Backfield Coaching Points:

Z —	Fake a stalk; run a go route.
X —	Radical inside release; run a climb post.
FB —	Seal C gap player.
TB —	Drop step; help C-to-D gaps.
QB —	Drop opposite foot two steps downhill; 5-step drop behind playside tackle's alignment.

4-3

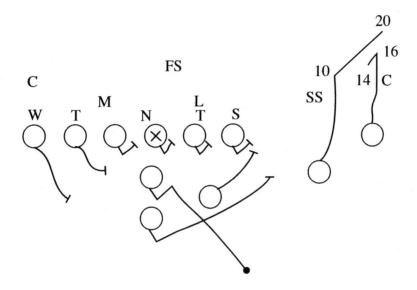

Blocking Rules:

Playside tackle —	Block 28/29.
Playside guard —	Block 28/29.
Center —	Block 28/29.
Backside guard —	Block 28/29.
Backside tackle —	Modify your 28/29 to a pass set drop.
Tight end —	Modify your 28/29 to a pass set drop.

Backfield Coaching Points:

Z —	Run a sail route 10-to-20 yards.
X —	Run a 16-to-14 yard stop hook.
FB —	Attack C gap; help splitside tackle.
TB —	Drop step; attack D gap.
QB —	Drop step two steps; 5-step set up behind playside tackle's alignment.

PLAY #98 — "DUO RIGHT 14 G PASS"

4-3

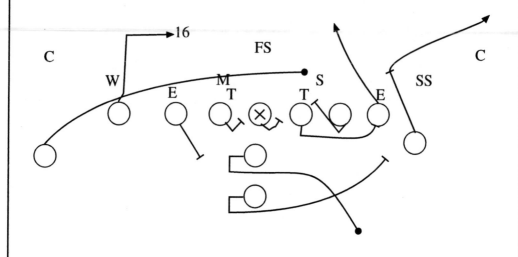

Blocking Rules:

Playside tackle — 14 G run rules.

Playside guard — Pull and log or kick out EMOL.

Center — Protect playside A gap.

Backside guard — Protect backside A gap, unless 3 technique; then do a modified pass drop.

Backside tackle — Modify your run rule to a pass set.

Tight end — Inside release; run centerfield; avoid contact.

Backfield Coaching Points:

Z - Run a dart route no deeper than six yards.

X - Come open late at 16 yards.

FB - Stalk corner.

TB - Whirly bird option; block C-to-D gap.

QB - Whirly bird option fake; two steps, 5-step drop behind P.S.T.'s alignment.

PLAY #99 — "TRIPS LEFT 18 FLOOD PASS"

4-3

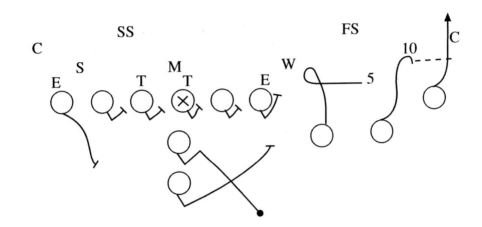

Blocking Rules:

Playside tackle —	Block 28/29.
Playside guard —	Block 28/29.
Center —	Block 28/29.
Backside guard —	Block 28/29.
Backside tackle —	Protect backside B gap, unless you have a 5 technique; then use a modified pass set.
Tight end —	Modify your 28/29 to a pass set drop.

Backfield Coaching Points:

Z —	Run a read curl/out at 16-to-18 yards; find a hole vs. zone; move vs. man.
X —	Run an outside release go route.
FB —	T-out route at five yards.
TB —	Drop step; help C gap; look for D gap rusher.
QB —	Drop step; take two steps; then slide to the flood side tackle's alignment.

PLAY #100 — "TRIPS LEFT 18 H SHALLOW PASS"

4-3

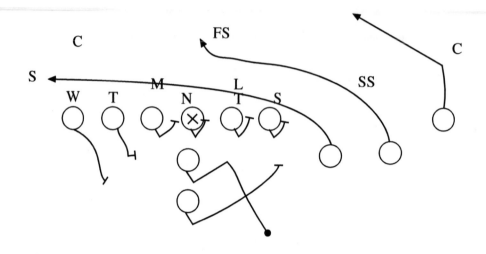

Blocking Rules:

Playside tackle —	Block 28/29.
Playside guard —	Block 28/29.
Center —	Block 28/29.
Backside guard —	Block 28/29.
Backside tackle —	Protect backside B gap unless 3 technique; then use a modified pass set.
Tight end —	Use a modified pass set to block edge rusher.

Backfield Coaching Points:

Z —	Run a thick post; get depth.
X —	Run a skinny post; get inside leverage on corner.
H —	Run a shallow cross no deeper than five yards.
TB —	Drop step; attack C gap to D gap.
QB —	Drop step; take two steps; set up behind P.S.T.'s alignment.

PLAY #101 — "ACE TREY RIGHT 18 Y SHALLOW PASS"

4-3

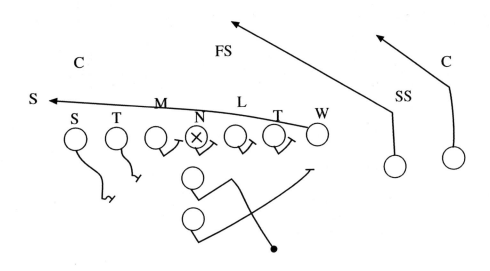

Blocking Rules:

Playside tackle —	Run a shallow cross no deeper than five yards.
Playside guard —	Block 28/29.
Center —	Block 28/29.
Backside guard —	Block 28/29.
Backside tackle —	Protect backside B gap, unless you have a 5 technique; then use a modified pass set.
Tight end —	Use a modified pass set to block edge.

Backfield Coaching Points:

Z —	Run a skinny post; get inside leverage on corner.
X —	Run a thick post; get depth.
FB —	Run 18 path; block C gap.
TB —	Drop step; attack C gap.
QB —	Drop step; set behind P.S.T. tackle.

ABOUT THE AUTHOR

Stan Zweifel is the assistant head football coach and offensive coordinator at the University of Wisconsin-Whitewater. Since joining the Warhawks staff in 1991, Zweifel has molded the UWW offensive team into one of two leading offenses in the nation. During that time, the Warhawks have been nationally ranked in the top 10 in rushing offense, scoring offense, total offense, and passing efficiency several times.

During his tenure, UWW has had 16 all-conference offensive players, five All-American players and seven players who have gone on to play professional football.

Stan has also authored three best-selling coaching books and has produced several well-received instructional videos on offensive football. Stan currently resides in Whitewater, Wisconsin with Diane, his wife of 25 years, and his children: daughters, Saree and Shannon, and sons, Michael and Mark.